POLSKIE TOW. KRAJOZNAWCZE · ODDZ

ZIEMIA ŁOMŻYŃSKA · BOŻNICA w ŚMIADO

TWO HITLERS
AND A MARILYN

TWO HITLERS
AND A MARILYN

Adam Andrusier

HEADLINE

First published in 2021 by
HEADLINE PUBLISHING GROUP

1

Please refer to page 306 for picture credits.

Cataloguing in Publication Data is available from the British Library

Hardback ISBN 978 1 4722 7708 4
Trade paperback ISBN 978 1 4722 7704 6

Designed and typeset by EM&EN
Printed and bound in Great Britain by Clays Ltd, Elcograf S.p.A.

Headline's policy is to use papers that are natural, renewable and recyclable
products and made from wood grown in well-managed forests and other
controlled sources. The logging and manufacturing processes are expected
to conform to the environmental regulations of the country of origin.

HEADLINE PUBLISHING GROUP
An Hachette UK Company
Carmelite House
50 Victoria Embankment
London EC4Y 0DZ

www.headline.co.uk
www.hachette.co.uk

For my mother and father,
and for my sister

Contents

Author's Note

Some details of this story have been altered,
including elements of characterization,
names, dates, places and events.

RONNIE BARKER

The marvellous thing about
a joke with a double meaning is that
it can only mean one thing.

Ronnie Barker

My father was the one behind the camera. One eye closed, half a smile, the rest of his face obscured by his Kodak. On every occasion there he'd be, clicking away like a paparazzo. The pictures came out blurred, or showed people sporting strange in-between expressions, but you couldn't knock his enthusiasm. If he took twenty snaps a day – a conservative estimate – that's 73,000 photos during the 1980s alone.

'Don't you want to have real experiences?' Mum would ask. 'Rather than just documenting everything?'

'I'm having experiences,' Dad disputed. 'I'm documenting them at the same time.'

My father had a penchant for a particular money shot: my mother, my sister and me in a dreary line.

'Come on,' he'd call out to us. 'Look happy!'

'We're trying. It's not easy.'

We bared our teeth in front of triptychs, on gondolas in Venice, beside Welcome to Wherever signs.

'You're a fantasist,' argued Mum. 'No one's going to look at all these photos.'

'*I'll* look at them. I want to have a record!'

In fact, what Dad mostly looked at was his collection of postcards of synagogues destroyed by the Nazis. Over bowls of Frosties my sister, Ruth, and I got minute-by-minute accounts of *Kristallnacht*, drawn from our father's vast library of books on Hitler, the Third Reich and genocide. Our games of Twister were interrupted by the death toll at

Treblinka. At weekends, Dad went to his study to take photographs of his synagogue postcards using a special mounted camera above the desk. The camera was a gift to himself for his fortieth birthday. He invited friends up there to watch him work. 'Very good, Adrian,' you heard them say. 'Nice to have a hobby.'

I asked Dad why he collected synagogues when we hardly ever went to Pinner United Synagogue.

'Because of continuity,' he said, flatly. 'These buildings were destroyed by Hitler. The ones that survived are now libraries and sports centres and cinemas. It's important to have a record.'

'Again, with the Nazis,' my mother called out from the kitchen. 'He's ten years old. Can you knock it off?'

One day, Dad decided to go through a box of his overflow family photos and cut out our faces with scissors. He found famous images in books, superimposed our faces, then took new pictures with his special camera. For example, a shot of Rudolf Nureyev dancing with Margot Fonteyn got Mum and Dad's faces superimposed. Or Fred Astaire and Ginger Rogers became me and my sister. Or the sailor kissing the girl in Times Square at the end of World War Two turned into Dad's accountant and his wife. We passed the study and heard the camera clicking and Dad laughing to himself as if he was the funniest man in the world. He got the images developed near his office and came home with a pile of 8×10-inch shiny prints that he peeled away, one by one, like a magician.

'It's perverse,' said Mum, turning to me, the ten-year old, for an explanation. 'Why would anyone do this?'

'Oh, it's just a bit of fun,' said Dad. 'How about this one?'

My sister and I as US marines, raising the Stars and Stripes at Iwo Jima.

'And this?'

My father's business partner, Michael Rose, delivering a speech at Nuremberg.

'And this is the one I'll use next!'

Dad flashed his prize possession at us – a hand-autographed photo of Danny Kaye, in character as Hans Christian Andersen, bought at one of his postcard fairs. 'Sincerely yours, Danny Kaye' it said in fountain pen ink. My father adored Danny Kaye and loved putting us in front of his films. Kaye was forever in excruciating situations, like having to perform impromptu ballets on stage, or pretending he was Irish, or having to climb through people's cars to get across a street. He did silly voices and embarrassed people – just like Dad. I liked Danny Kaye but also pitied him because he was always such a first-class shmuck.

'I plan to use this on top.'

Dad moved his own cut-out face – sporting a false Hassidic beard – into position over Danny Kaye's.

'I think you need help,' said Mum.

§

The first time I asked for an autograph I surprised even myself; a weird accident. It was while I was at Adam Brichto's house. Adam was my best friend when I was ten years old. He lived in a white house on Amberley Close. It had a row of columns at the front as if it was the entrance to Roman baths. Our house was covered top to bottom in thick brown carpet, but the Brichtos' was cream and everything looked as if it had just been polished by the au pair, Astrid, who was always hoovering and piling up clothes. Adam's dad was a rabbi at the Liberal synagogue and had an office at the front of the house that we weren't allowed into. Everything was calm at the Brichtos'. Adam's dad kept himself to himself. He didn't collect things or ask people to look at photos or do impressions of SS officers.

Mostly what Adam and I did was play marbles. The two of us would start off in his bedroom then graduate to the rest of the house, ending up gently chastised by Adam's mum, or by Astrid. One day, when Rabbi Brichto was out at work and Adam's mum busy on the phone, we couldn't resist extending our game into the front office. Our marbles raced towards it, and we opened the door.

My own dad's study had books and papers everywhere, and smelt musty, and according to Mum resembled Dresden after the bombings. By contrast, Adam's dad's office had white floor-to-ceiling shelving units with books neatly stacked. On the presidential desk at the centre were silver-framed photographs of Rabbi Brichto at black-tie events, standing next to important-looking people. In one, he was shown laughing next to the actual prime minister. I examined that photo carefully to check Adam's dad hadn't superimposed his own face from another picture.

'Your dad knows Maggie Thatcher?' I asked.

'Oh, he met her once,' said Adam's mum, appearing in the doorway. 'He's met a few famous people.'

Adam's mum wasn't annoyed we'd found our way into her husband's study, but then she was good-natured, pretty and slim. She called me 'Adam A' and her own son 'Adam B'. When Adam refused to eat a vegetable, she'd play-act with him and make us both laugh. 'But if you don't try it, Adam B, I'm going to have to cry,' she'd say, with a pretend crying voice. Then, 'You're being mean to me! Why do you have to be so mean, Adam B?' Adam's mum was forever drying her hair or getting dressed to go out somewhere. If, during dinner, the phone rang, she'd take off an earring to answer it, then hold the receiver for a long time, laughing and gossiping with a friend. When I told Mum about that on the way home, she said it was wrong, that if someone phoned you during dinner you should call them back later.

'Did Adam B tell you we have Ronnie Barker living round the corner?' asked Adam's mum.

Incredible news. My family didn't do many things the whole country did, but we did, like the country, sit down together on Saturday evenings to watch *The Two Ronnies*. Even my grandparents enjoyed it. 'This Ronnie Barker,' my grandfather would say in his Czech accent, wagging a finger. 'He knows a thing or two. Very clever.' The idea of someone as famous as Ronnie Barker living close by to Adam Brichto felt spooky to me, like the strangest bit of good luck.

'He's over the road, on Moss Lane,' said Adam's mum.

When she left the room, I said, 'Does Ronnie Barker *really* live round the corner? Or was your mum joking?'

'It's true,' said Adam. 'Come on. Let's see if we can spot him!'

We told Adam's mum we were going to play football at the front of the house. She was in the kitchen preparing a salad and said it was fine, so long as we were careful. We slammed the front door shut, sneaked out to the end of Amberley Close and took a sharp right onto Moss Lane.

'Won't your mum check up on us, and see we've gone?' I asked. I imagined my own mother having a heart attack.

'She won't notice,' said Adam. 'She'll be on the phone.'

'But do you even know which house it is?'

I was breathy with excitement as we made our way down leafy Moss Lane, past the red telephone box and the bench.

'It's the one on the corner, with all the trees.'

We crossed the road, then Adam B slowed his step.

'Here. This is the one,' he said.

We were standing beside a shoulder-height fence which had entangled plants above it, making it hard to see any-thing, so we had to push our faces right into the shrubbery. Instantly, we saw the back of an old man's head through the bay window. He was seated in a chair and talking to another man standing a few feet away. He turned his head to one side.

'Oh my God, I think it's him!' I exclaimed.

'It is him! It is!' shouted Adam.

But something wasn't right. The man who was wearing the grey pullover looked tired. His face was solemn and impatient. He wasn't laughing or making the other man laugh.

'Are you sure?' I asked.

I stared as hard as I could and tried to square this person with the man who came onto our television at weekends. The man on TV looked generous and hearty. This guy wasn't even wearing the trademark glasses that spun around in ani-mation at the start of the show.

'It must be him,' said Adam B, straining to see.

'Let's knock on the door!' I yelped.

'Yeah, good idea.'

We banged the heavy knocker and looked at each other as if we were bank robbers. We couldn't believe we'd done it. There was a glass panel which was wonky and warped so you couldn't see the person's face on the other side, but you could see their shadow approaching. I held my breath. Oh my God, oh my God, oh my God.

The door opened, but it wasn't Ronnie Barker. It was a woman. She looked startled.

'Does Ronnie Barker live here?' asked Adam Brichto, abruptly.

'Yes, he does,' said the woman.

'Can we meet him?'

'I'm sorry,' said the woman, 'but he doesn't see people at the door.'

Which is the moment when, for some reason, Dad's signed photo of Danny Kaye came to mind, with the flowing ink signature.

I said, 'But we want to get his autograph.'

'I'm sorry. Not at the door. That's not possible. Why don't you write to him, instead?'

I tried to see past the woman in case Ronnie Barker was in the hallway behind her, about to change his policy. But before I knew it, the door was closed shut again.

'Oh well,' I said to Adam, as we walked back to his house. 'At least we saw him.'

'Yeah, but he looked weird,' said Adam B. 'He didn't look famous at all.'

That night, I told my mum what had happened, expecting her to ask questions, like why hadn't we had an adult with us, and had we been safe? Instead, she said, 'Oh, I do like

Ronnie Barker. He's very clever. You should do what the woman said. You should write to him. Tell him how much you enjoy his programme.'

So, I put pen to paper. If I couldn't meet the man, I figured at the very least I could have a record of him.

> *Dear Ronnie Barker*
>
> *I was one of the boys who knocked on your door today.*
> *Would it be possible for you to send me your autograph?*
> *I'd love to have it. I think you are one of the funniest,*
> *cleverest people on television. My whole family watches you*
> *every Saturday night.*
>
> *Yours hopefully,*
>
> *Adam Andrusier*

Mum posted it the next day.

On the first evening, I put an episode of *The Two Ronnies* on our Betamax video. While I watched the silly sketches, I thought of my letter and felt a special connection with Ronnie Barker that set me apart from my parents and sister. It was as if he was now mine – no longer theirs, or the country's. I was swept away by a feeling that something amazing had been set in motion.

Each day, the postman came at the same time, 8 a.m., just before I left for school. While my father vigorously brushed his corkscrew locks in the front hall mirror and my sister dried her tangle of curls upstairs, I positioned myself in our bay window and waited to see the first red fleck of the postman's shoulder bag at the end of our street. I crouched down as he picked his way along, house by house, till he came to our pathway. The click of the letterbox went, and I darted across the carpet then rifled through all the bills and boring letters addressed to my stupid parents. Each day the same routine, and each day nothing.

On the fourth day, the letterbox clinked and a letter arrived hand-addressed to me. It was the same envelope I'd sent to Ronnie Barker, but his name and address had been crossed out and someone had written mine instead. I ripped it open, and a small colour photograph dropped onto the brown carpet. I held it carefully between my fingers and tilted it in the light, just the way my dad would do with his special photos. It was a picture of Ronnie Barker in his trade-mark glasses, looking exactly the way he did on television, grinning madly. On the photo in black ink it said, 'For Adam, with best wishes, Ronnie Barker.'

'Gosh, that's very nice of him,' said Mum, 'considering you knocked on his door unannounced.'

'Amazing,' said my dad, blinking his eyes but not concentrating well.

'Aren't you surprised he sent a photo?' I asked.

I was trying to distract my father, who was frantically searching for something in his briefcase.

'Now, look, I'm sorry to interrupt,' said Dad. 'But you must just see *this*.'

He withdrew from his briefcase the reproduced 8×10 print of Danny Kaye as Hans Christian Andersen. But, wait. It didn't have Dad's head superimposed, as promised. It had mine!

'What do you think?' Dad pouted with suppressed hilarity.

I had a bad feeling in my stomach, and offered a pained smile. My superimposed face fake-smiled back at me, and I remembered exactly where that shot had been taken. Under the Arc de Triomphe in ninety-degree heat when we'd all lost the will to live, but Dad kept on snapping. 'Another one! This way! One more! *I want a record!*'

BIG DADDY

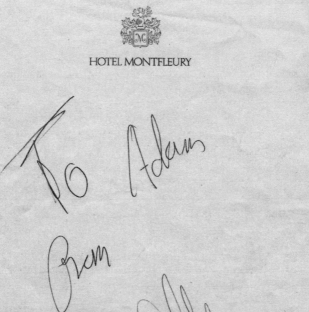

HOTEL MONTFLEURY

To Adam

from

Big Daddy

25, AVENUE BEAUSÉJOUR, 06409 CANNES ★ TÉLÉPHONE: (93) 68.91.50 ★ TÉLEX: 470039

After a while,
I started to get very angry.
The desire to defend myself
became overwhelming.

Big Daddy

Throughout the 1980s my father suffered from a chronic case of sixties mania. The Profumo scandal, the disastrous arrival of Yoko Ono on the scene and the early death of Eddie Cochran were his live concerns. He talked incessantly about those years. 'Do you remember . . .?' he asked friends in a rhetorical tone. Our family parties were sixties themed. Rock 'n' roll quizzes were a fixture.

Dad used our Betamax video to record anything that came on about that era, including a documentary in several parts, *The History of Rock 'n' Roll*, which we watched together as a family. Dad delivered side-lectures. At weekends, he stuck on sixties music and twitched his hand in my mother's direction, and my sister and I would make demented faces at each other while our parents danced. Dad grabbed his curls with one hand, spread the other across his skinny belly and popped his body around like he was a chicken.

In the Volvo during school run he became particularly excitable. He forced us to listen to his favourite songs from the Hit Parade and stroked my cheeks while they played. 'You like it, Adam be-doobee-doobs?' he asked. I nodded, then tried putting on one of my own cassettes of the Eurythmics or Prince or 'Free Nelson Mandela'. But Dad was having none of it.

'Not really my thing,' he said, pressing the eject button.

He fumbled again with his own cassettes till a stuttering voice came through the speakers, something about a pretty girl named Peggy Sue, then Dad started thrusting his chin back and forth.

'Buddy Holly died in a plane crash. Completely tragic. I remember it like it was yesterday.'

In traffic jams in Kenton my sister and I got after-dinner speeches about the Cuban Missile Crisis, the Six Day War, Kennedy's assassination. We also got lectures on how poor Dad's family had been, how he'd slept in the lounge, how there was a time they'd been evicted. And now – look at him! – driving a Volvo 760, with electric roof and seats that warmed up when you pressed the red button. We drove along the Hendon Way with the windows down, boosting out 'Love Potion Number Nine'.

'Where shall we go on holiday this summer, Doobs?' asked Dad.

'California!'

I called to mind cardboard cut-outs of Charles and Diana in the back windows of our hire car, people yelling 'My God! Your accents!' and 'How's the fog in London, these days?' One person asked if we personally knew Patrick Macnee of *The Avengers*. 'We don't know him, but we know who he is,' replied Dad, wagging a finger. Then the boat trip in Disneyland where the figures stood on the banks, singing and dancing, changing nationality. My sister and I felt like a king and queen surveying our kingdom. 'It's a world of laughter, a world of tears, it's a small world after all.'

As we circled Northwick Park roundabout, Dad laughed and said, 'You want to go again?'

'Yes! Can we?'

'We'll see.'

I shut my eyes for a bit and listened to the music, feeling like I was part of Dad's new and luxurious lifestyle, and that everything would always be fine – just as long as Yoko Ono didn't come and screw things up again.

§

My father was a financial advisor and life insurance broker, which meant he advised people on how to bet against their own deaths. He couldn't technically stop you from dying but could help you mitigate against it financially, as long as you didn't mind being dead when the policy paid out. 'All I know,' he said, 'is I get a lot of letters from widows thanking me for the advice I gave their late husbands.'

His office was on Regent Street above a jewellery shop. I always spent a day there during the school holidays. Dad bounced in brandishing postcards of lost synagogues. He stroked the secretaries' cheeks and told a bad Englishman, Irishman and Scotsman joke before asking his main secretary, Trisha, 'Would you like to make some tea, Bubbles?' Her eyes widened as Dad fondled her face, and I nodded empathetically, conveying *Stay strong, Trisha – we can get through this together*.

Then Dad would turn to me and stroke *my* cheeks like I was a hamster, which made it Trisha's turn to nod knowingly.

'This is my son,' Dad announced to his staff. 'My *son!*'

'We know, Adrian,' the staff replied. 'We've met him before.'

My father's office walls teemed with faded prints of cartoon characters making jokes about dying, scattered paper and calculators on the desks, plus a cracked framed photograph of Dad as Charlton Heston as Moses receiving the Ten Commandments. The main thing, though, was the files. There were heaps of them everywhere, with clients' names scrawled on in block capitals: files on the floor, files on the windowsills, files on the chairs too, including where the client was meant to sit. If Dad's study at home conveyed the abandoned ruins of Dresden, his office spoke of the littered, bleached wastelands of Hiroshima.

'Where's Howard Spiegel's file?' Dad bellowed.

'Maybe among these?' A forlorn-looking secretary appeared holding yet more files.

'It's not there,' Dad barked, continuing his frenzied search. 'Ah, it's alright, Bubbles. I've found it!'

Going to Dad's office during the school holidays was billed as "fun". As soon as we arrived, Dad forgot I existed. I was left to my own devices while he spun in his director's chair, signing documents with a flourish. I figured my sister, Ruth, had made the better choice, ensconced in our living room at home reading the works of Dickens, Mum hoovering around her.

Sometimes a shiny-looking client arrived for an appointment, all smiles and handshakes and 'How are you, Adrian?' Dad told them the same joke he'd told the secretaries earlier, then pointed at me and said, 'That's my son.' I flicked a smile as he disappeared into his office. Then, within seconds, he pressed a button on his phone and said to whichever secretary answered, 'Bubbles, you couldn't get me a quote on Mr Goldfarb's joint life first-death policy, could you?' I watched the secretary raise her eyes to heaven at the sound of Dad's voice, then go in and fake-smile as if she was posing for one of his photos.

Dad must have told Trisha about my autograph of Ronnie

Barker, because she had an idea about how I could get more. She went through all the listings in the *Evening Standard* to see which actors were appearing on stage.

'You can write to them care of the theatres,' she suggested.

'But can you tell me which ones are really famous?' I demanded.

'You're the boss's son,' Trisha winked. 'I'll do my best.'

We were soon interrupted by Dad's voice, calling out something about total and permanent disability, and Trisha would say, 'Gotta go, darling. Dad needs me,' then she disappeared. She sat at her desk typing letters at a hundred words a minute with her headset on so she could hear my father's recorded voice; I saw her pause to shake out her fingers. Meanwhile, I handwrote letter after letter to actors I'd never heard of, essentially bored out of my brains against the backdrop of Trisha's typing, and my father composing yet more letters on his Dictaphone. Full stop. New paragraph.

At lunchtime, Dad remembered I existed. He poked his head around his door and grinned. 'So, Adam be-doobee-doobs. Shall we take a walk down Carnaby Street, my son?'

Once we were walking, it was like the bit at the office had never happened. We strolled down Regent Street and he told me how good it felt to have an office right in the centre of things. And, some day, perhaps I'd like to join his company?

'Not really my thing.'

'Well, you're young, Doobs. There's time. Who knows what you'll end up doing? Frankly, there are so many things I could have done, myself, besides insurance. For instance, I'd have made a great film director.'

In Carnaby Street, Dad shook his head at the T-shirts with Hitler's face on – 'World Tour 1939–1945' – and frowned at the punks with long boots, studs in their faces, and huge coloured, pointy hairdos.

'They remind me of Toyah,' I commented, thinking of the scary orange hair I'd seen on *Top of the Pops.*

'Who?'

'Toyah, Dad. Don't you know who she is? She's a famous pop star!'

'Oh, I'm not following the pop music,' explained Dad. 'Which reminds me. Have you heard of a band called the Thompson Twins?'

'Thompson Twins? Of course, I have!'

'Well, I've got Tony Smith coming in next week – an accountant friend of mine – and he's going to introduce them, in case they want some insurance. I'll ask for their autographs, shall I? I want to help you build your collection.'

'Really? That would be amazing.'

I pretty much forgot about the Thompson Twins thing because I was busy writing to actors I'd never heard of. I wrote to people called Alan Bates, Ben Kingsley, Michael Gambon, Helen Mirren, Antony Sher and Bonnie Langford. I wrote so many letters I got cramp in my hand, just like Trisha, and had to stop to massage my fingers.

'I've got a present for you,' said Dad, one evening.

He produced a colourful record from a plastic bag. The Thompson Twins were posed at different angles like Dr Seuss characters, and each one had signed the record cover in silver ink adding a special message to me.

'Wow. Thanks!'

I couldn't believe my father had met these actual people, and that they'd signed their names for me. I stared at all the handwriting – the 'love always' and 'lotsa fun' – as if they were ancient runes that needed decoding.

'I must say, I hadn't expected there to be three of them,' said Dad. 'Can't imagine why they call themselves twins.'

It was an exciting addition to my burgeoning autograph collection, but also the first record I'd owned, so I put it on all the time. I paid close attention to the spread piano chords, the squelchy low-down baseline and echoey castanets in the introduction before anyone started singing, 'Hold me now, warm my heart, stay with me, let loving start.' I had no idea what the song was about, but it didn't matter. The woman with the shaved head was the girlfriend of the one with the brown spiky hair, Dad explained, which made me wonder if they might be about to start building a pension pot together. I figured the one with the long spiky black hair was probably after critical illness cover.

'They liked me,' Dad added.

Not long after, my father came home with amazing news. He'd been right about the Thompson Twins liking him, because now they'd invited him and Mum to a party in the countryside.

'I'm not going,' said Mum. 'I can't do the whole insurance broker's wife thing.'

'Oh, come on, Lo-lo. It'll be fun.'

'Will you get autographs?' I gasped. 'There'll be loads of pop stars there!'

'Oh, I suppose,' said Dad. 'I'll definitely try.'

*

As the night of the party approached, I had the whole thing planned out. My father would basically work the room and get every famous signature going. I coached him on how to interrupt celebrity conversations.

'Don't let me down,' I warned.

It didn't seem fair when Mum and Dad disappeared off in the Volvo for their pop star party in the countryside, while Ruth and I were left to play Monopoly with the babysitter and watch the *Saturday Show*, where Big Daddy threw Giant Haystacks around a wrestling ring, followed by *3-2-1*, where the contestants crashed out with Dusty Bin. But I went to bed without a fuss that night because I couldn't wait to wake up the next morning and see what my father had brought back.

'It was incredible,' said Dad. 'There were jugglers and magicians and midgets serving drinks and fireworks and all sorts. I don't think I've ever seen a house that big. Mummy thought it was flashy, but I loved it.'

'And who was there, Dad? Which pop stars?'

'Oh, there was somebody George.'

'Not *Boy* George?' I gasped. 'You got his autograph?'

'That was it – Boy George. And Lionel Richie was there. And a girl band.'

'Which one?' I was mentally inserting all the new signatures into my collector's album.

Dad called out to Mum, who was still in bed, 'What was the name of that girl band, Anna?'

'Bananarama,' Mum called out.

That made even my sister emerge from her bedroom, clutching her Charlotte Brontë.

'*Bananarama?*' we both shrieked.

'I don't know them,' said Dad.

'So, you got me autographs. Please show me the autographs!'

'Oh, I'm sorry,' said Dad, sadly. 'I couldn't. I tried to get near Lionel Richie, but it was impossible. And I wasn't completely sure which one Boy George was. And even though I was standing right next to Bananarama, I didn't find out who they were until later. Tony Smith told me – the Thompson Twins' accountant.'

I was devastated. A one-off opportunity, and my father had screwed it up. I pictured him at the party, talking to boring accountants about pension pots and Yoko Ono while all the crazy partying went on around him. I couldn't understand why he hadn't tried harder. Imagining my father at the Thompson Twins' party made me see him differently; it made me see him as smaller.

§

Not long after, on a week's holiday in the South of France, I came face to face with the most famous person of all time. Ruth and I were swimming in the pool when I noticed a huge man on one of the balconies doing vigorous exercises. He was fat and blond and bobbing his head up and down. He looked enormously strong. And familiar. When he paused, he came into focus.

'Oh my God!' I yelled at my sister. 'It's Big Daddy!'

We stared for a while, but he disappeared from view, back into his bedroom. He looked so much stronger than on television, which made me wonder how my own father would fare in a fight with him. Big Daddy would snap him in half.

My mum suggested I get a piece of hotel-headed paper and a pen just in case Big Daddy came down to the pool. And, later that day, he appeared. He was tall and hugely fat, and walked like a titan. His biceps were easily three times the size of Dad's, and his enormous swimming trunks went in a big circle around his belly. When he dropped into the pool, the water rose up around him like he was a hippopotamus. I got ready with my pen and paper. I felt nervous about approaching the megastar but decided I couldn't be like my dad at the Thompson Twins' party. I had to succeed.

Eventually, the wrestler got tired of swimming and eased himself slowly up the pool steps.

'Are you Big Daddy?' I asked.

'For my sins,' he said, smiling. 'What's your name?'

'Adam. Can I have your autograph?'

'Course you can, son. Let me lean on your back.'

I turned around, and the huge man placed the piece of paper on me and started to write, then he said, 'There you go.'

He'd written, 'To Adam from Big Daddy.'

I took the piece of paper back to my parents, waving it over my head like a golden Wonka ticket.

'Look,' I said, trying to catch my father's eye. '*That's* how you do it!'

'Marvellous,' said Mum, looking up from her Latin cross-word. 'Well done.'

'I got a couple of snaps,' said Dad, tapping his camera beside him on the sun lounger. 'My God, the man's enormous. He'll have a heart attack if he's not careful.'

'Maybe you should sell him some life insurance,' suggested Mum in a quiet voice.

Dad rearranged his sinewy, svelte body on the lounger and smiled up at the sun. 'Which reminds me of that joke. What do you call a woman who knows where her husband is all the time?'

'Dunno,' we said.

'A widow.'

Dad smirked at his own punchline, then patted his bare chest with a flat hand.

'I've heard that joke at least a hundred times,' said Mum.

'You know, it was more about boxing in my day,' Dad continued, as if responding to a question by an interviewer. 'The Henry Cooper fight against Muhammad Ali in 1963. What a fight that was. Can't say I remember any *wrestling*.'

I was trying to tune my father out by staring at the hand-writing on the page and its message to me.

'Oh, and Doobs,' Dad said, turning his head on the head-rest and lowering his voice, 'you do know that Big Daddy isn't his real name? His real name's Shirley Crabtree. Shirley! Can you believe it?'

'Huh,' I said. 'Almost as bad as Adrian.'

'Adrian's not bad, is it?' Dad seemed suddenly anxious and half sat up.

'It's not the best,' said Mum.

But Big Daddy wasn't Shirley Crabtree. He was Big Daddy. He'd looked like him, he'd behaved like him, and he'd written his name on my piece of paper. I'd managed to puncture a hole between our universe and the parallel one where all the celebrities lived, and I wasn't going to let my father spoil that. And I definitely wasn't going to end up spinning in an office chair, muttering into a Dictaphone, sending point-less letters and making secretaries' eyes roll. For the rest of the holiday, that chance encounter by the pool was pretty much all I thought about. I knew that when we got home and Dad was stuck on a sixties theme, and turning down the volume of 'California Dreamin'' to inform me that Mama Cass had choked to death on a ham sandwich, I had a story of my own tucked away to tell my own children some day. A story that had happened right now in the eighties.

SINATRA

Strange, but I feel the
world we live in demands that
we be turned out in a pattern
which resembles, in fact, *is*
a facsimile of itself.

Frank Sinatra

When Esztergom synagogue got speared by Adam Brichto's stray dart, Dad relocated us to the garage. He set up the board among crate-loads of crockery, candlesticks and worthless pots.

'There. Knock yourselves out,' he barked, and went to attend to his ailing synagogue.

Adam and I threw some twos and threes, then missed the board altogether. One dart landed in a dustbin bag in the far corner. When Adam B went to retrieve it, he got an eyeful of some of the biggest tits, cocks and widespread arse-cheeks ever committed to print.

'Oh my God, what's this?' he asked, holding up a shot of a woman displaying two enormous appendages next to her cheeks, like earrings.

I hurried over to see what the fuss was about.

'Why's that nurse sitting on her patient's face?' I asked.

We were turning the pages of a luridly coloured magazine titled *Barely Eighteen*. I was barely eleven myself, but pretty sure this was not standard hospital procedure.

'Weird,' said Adam, giggling. 'Some of them have stories, too – look.'

We read through together, trying our best to concentrate on the narrative. There was a real cliffhanger about two women – Freja and Laura – being picked up by two men they'd never met before and spending a fun day at the Tivoli Gardens, before returning to Freja's apartment to spend the next three hours 'having their cunts fucked so many times by

Bjorn and Sven that cum was running down their thighs, dripping down onto their knickers and covering them all in sticky goo'.

'Gross,' said Adam B, fast-flicking the pages of a small red booklet. 'Look at this one. Two men pissing in her mouth!'

'Wow,' I said. 'Can she be enjoying that?'

'She looks pretty pleased with herself.'

'Fake smile, though,' I asserted. 'This one's real. Look.'

A middle-aged woman grinning like a lottery winner while a second woman stuck a cucumber into her bottom.

'You're right,' said Adam. 'She looks delighted.'

'Quick! Put them back,' I instructed. 'Mum's coming.'

For the next six months, every time Adam Brichto came over we went to the garage to lose darts and stare at photos of orgies, anal plugs and 69ers. When we got bored of Freja and Laura's Tivoli antics, we discovered other stories. Like a nun visiting a priest for confession and ending up in a threesome with the choirmaster.

'Fake,' said Adam B, pointing at the nun's oddly flared nostrils.

'I don't know,' I said. 'Fifty-fifty. Her eyes are smiling.'

I wasn't certain why we wanted to look at these images, and felt hesitant, not least because these women were doing things Mum would disapprove of. She didn't even like people kissing on television. 'What bothers me is the pretending,' she used to say. 'They're actors.' Dad would shrug in disagreement: 'You never know – they might be enjoying it.' Then Mum would switch channels. I figured, if she didn't like Dad watching kissing, there was no way she'd want him staring at pictures of women measuring black cocks.

Dad was transgressing Mum's rules, I decided, abusing

her trust. Like an amateur sleuth, I began watching the man for other signs of duplicity. Storing spare light bulbs in the garage? Who was he kidding? I found I paid careful attention now to his twitchy shoulders when 'Sexual Healing' played in the car. I combed through Dad's bedside table and held up sweet wrappers to the light in case they'd been indented with secret messages from porn stars. I took regular breaks from my detective work to practise my darts.

§

By the mid-1980s, I'd had it with theatre actors. Occasionally, people made other suggestions, like try writing to Jimmy Savile at Stoke Mandeville Hospital or Rolf Harris at the Norfolk and Norwich, where they cheer up the children. Rolf sent me a drawing of himself as a kangaroo, and Jimmy sent a charming note, turning the 'S' of his name into a dollar sign. These successes were pleasing, but I needed to spread my net wider. The problem was, how to find the famous people's addresses? I couldn't very well wait to bump into them in swimming pools in the South of France.

One day, Dad had a thought. He disappeared into his study, and after a lot of groaning and throwing paper around he emerged clutching a brightly illustrated brochure. I did a double take – it looked like the cover of *Color Climax*. It was, in fact, a "Beverly Hills Star Map".

'I'd forgotten all about this,' he gleamed. 'Might be useful.'

That map was more than useful. It had little stars that showed you *exactly* where the old-timers lived. I remembered, now, how we'd used the map on our trip in California. We'd seen hedges trimmed at Gene Kelly's residence and watched a man in overalls arriving at Spielberg's place with a pot plant. Other than a torn, missing corner, they were all right there, and now I knew how to find them.

I deluged Beverly Hills with letters of admiration.

'Who's Fred Gwynne?' I demanded of Dad, raising my voice over the Supremes. 'Is he famous?'

'Yes. The one from whatchamacallit – *The Munsters*.'

'What about Dick Sargent – who's he? And Dom DeLuise?'

'I don't know those two. But have you thought about writing to James Cagney? A huge star! And Phil Silvers?'

A few weeks later, the first Hollywood autograph arrived: a large photo of James Cagney, showing him anciently old, and signed in a shaky hand, 'To Adam, Jim Cagney.'

'But is that actually him?' Mum queried. 'He looks like a prune.'

'The man's eighty-five years old,' Dad reasoned.

Other signed photos came in from James Stewart, Kirk Douglas and Gene Kelly; smiling, glamorous shots arrived from Lauren Bacall, Eva Marie Saint, Kim Novak and Hedy Lamarr.

'Ooh, Lauren Bacall was lovely,' said Dad. 'And did you know Hedy Lamarr was the first actress to appear completely naked on screen?' He pursed his lips and blinked a lot.

'All fake,' adjudicated Adam Brichto when he came over, pulling his finger across the line of breezy smiles.

The biggest success, though, was the megastar Frank Sinatra. He'd been missing from the map – presumably in the torn-off corner – so I'd addressed an envelope simply, 'Frank Sinatra, U.S.A.' Dad said I didn't stand a chance in hell. Not only did Frank get my letter, but he sent a colour photo of himself singing, and in silver ink he wrote, 'Sincerely yours, Frank Sinatra'. My father was gobsmacked by this achievement, and even though I hadn't ever seen any of Sinatra's films or heard him sing a single note, that one became my favourite. I separated it from the main collection and Blu-tacked it to my bedroom wall. When parents' friends came over, Dad would say, 'Go on, Doobs, show them the Sinatra,' as if that photo had become "ours".

While I was grateful for the autographs I got, I thought mostly about the ones that seemed unobtainable, like mean old Danny Kaye, who never replied, and stingy Charles Schulz, who was always too busy to draw a lousy Snoopy. Katharine Hepburn wasn't playing ball, either. She had a smug secretary reply on her behalf: 'I'm sorry, but Miss Hepburn doesn't sign or send autographs.' I'd write back, detailing the graphic extent of my admiration. 'I'm sorry,' came the next reply, 'but it's Miss Hepburn's policy not to sign autographs for people she doesn't know.' Miss Hepburn didn't know me? I'd written nine times.

'If it's addresses you're after, why not try the *Who's Who*?' suggested Dad's business partner one evening, as he thought-lessly creased my Sinatra.

'What's that?' I prised the photo out of the insurance salesman's hand.

'It's a big red book,' explained Dad, 'full of famous people's biographies.'

My father had failed to inform me of a book filled with the addresses of famous people?

'Sorry, Doobs. I forgot.'

That's about right, I thought. You didn't forget to sub-
scribe to *Girls Who Crave Big Cocks*, though.

After school, I stopped off at Pinner library and spent hours
flicking through the *Who's Who*, trying to decide who was
famous enough to write to. I was looking for real greatness,
now – the trailblazers; the people who'd brushed with history
and done more than set up whole-of-life death benefits for
their children. I wrote charming letters and got creative with
the truth. I figured it wouldn't hurt if I made myself younger
than I was, in the eight-to-ten bracket, and it was probably
good to appear to want to pursue a career path identical to
said famous person. I worked out a killer sentence to put at
the end of each letter, which went, 'You may not realize how
much it would mean to me to have your autograph.'

Signed photos arrived from Neil Armstrong in his spacesuit, Eric Clapton stroking his guitar and Mikhail Kalashnikov
manhandling a massive gun. At weekends, I showed the new
arrivals to Dad, imitating his magician style, peeling them
away one by one. It made him terribly nostalgic, but I denied
him his usual diatribes; five seconds per photo, ten seconds
each for my autograph letters from David Attenborough,
Margot Fonteyn and General Pinochet, all of whom were
delighted I'd be following in their professional footsteps.

Dad got more and more excited by the collection I was
building and threw out names during the day. 'Christine
Keeler!' he shouted from the bath, and 'What about Evel
Knievel?', as if he and I were inviting celebrities to a big party
in the countryside where the famous people would be entertained by sword-swallowing dwarfs while we talked shop
with accountants.

When the postman came at 8 a.m., there was now invariably something for me.

'Pfff, Kirk Douglas,' I'd grimace.

'You have him already?' Dad would ask.

'My fourth. The man signs everything. I was hoping for the Pope.'

§

Dad went to postcard fairs on the last Sunday of each month to look for photographs of synagogues and people standing around – what he termed the 'Jewish street life' part of his collection. The fairs took place in a hotel in Bloomsbury and involved him getting up ultra-early to see off his main rival. I pictured a wizened army general with a bayonet until Dad revealed one day it was a GP from Finchley by the name of Dr Levy. Levy had a big collection of synagogues, and an even larger one of Anti-Semitica – my father screwed up his face as he told me. At midday, Dad would be home again with rare cards and stories of astonishing pricing errors by the traders.

'Some of them have autographs of dead people,' Dad informed me one Sunday, with a glint in his eye. 'And there's a dealer called Sig Bernstein who *specializes* in autographs – mostly vintage Hollywood. You should come along next month and show him your collection.'

Now, dead autographs; that was an interesting proposition. Not least because I was fast running out of alive people to write to.

'Reserve me a seat in the Volvo,' I instructed.

En route to the fair, over the 'Ba-ba-ba' drone of the Beach Boys, Dad coached me on how to hunt effectively.

'If they've got an autograph you want, act casual,' he advised. 'Make them think you already have it, then you can negotiate.'

'I see,' I said, noting this new example of Dad's duplicity.

'And try to make them like you – that gives you an edge on your competitors. They might hold cards for you the next time around. But it's unpredictable.' Dad shook his head as if reporting on some fledgling democracy in East Africa.

'Right-o. Good luck,' said Dad when we arrived at the fair.

It seemed we'd be fighting this war in separate battalions. My father disappeared very quickly down an aisle.

The stalls mostly had large wooden crates on the tables filled with postcards marked into different themes. There were golf cards, glamour, military, churches, railways, religion, tennis. You could hear collectors announcing themselves at the stalls. 'I'm looking for Cyprus,' one swarthy individual explained. 'Anything new in balloonists?' asked a man with a squeaky voice.

'Autographs? Too difficult,' was the response I mostly got. Some dealers said, 'Try Music Hall', then I'd flick through ancient posed images of jugglers and children dressed as angels, and long-deceased husband and wife duos rubbing cheeks. Certain names came up again and again, like George Robey and Marie Lloyd and Gracie Fields, and sometimes you'd see a signature in very old, faded fountain pen ink with a personal message to a Lillian, Maud or Cyril. It was hard to believe any of these people had ever existed, never mind entertained anyone, what with their top hats, po-faces and frilly blouses. They were all so incredibly dead.

One lively dealer produced an album that had a series of 5×7 signed photographs of the old-timers, with names I recognized. There was a photo of Betty Grable signed in bright red ink, a young-looking James Cagney, Boris Karloff and Alan Ladd, all signed in flowing fountain pen. My father passed by and insisted on buying Betty Grable, because it was only £10 and she had million-dollar legs. The dealer put the Grable into a paper bag, and I clutched her to my chest. It gave me a peculiar sensation: the joining up of the living with the dead.

'I've found some fantastic cards,' Dad said. 'The interior of Kraków synagogue. Very rare. And this postcard of Kato-wice synagogue. Never seen it.' Dad held the cards very close to his face, as if he wanted to eat them. 'It's a wonderful feeling, you know, rescuing something, bearing witness to a Jewish life that once existed. This synagogue was set on fire by the Nazis in 1939.'

'What about that dealer you told me about? Sig Bern-stein. Is he here?'

I wanted to see autographs of megastars, plus I had my whole collection in my bag, and was keen to show it off.

'Yes, I saw him, Doobs. Come on.'

Sig Bernstein turned out to be a very small man in a short-sleeved shirt with skinny, floppy arms – like Popeye, but before the spinach. He had a gruff, deep voice and didn't smile, yet acted like he was well used to an appreciative audience.

'I've got everything,' he barked. He had a strong Ameri-can accent, and halitosis to sink a ship. 'Hepburn, Gable, the Marx Brothers, Harlow. You name it. Show your son.'

He stood with his arms folded at the front of his stall, as if barring access to illicit goods, then stepped furtively aside while screwing up his eyes at something in the distance – the flash of a police badge? I began flicking through his vintage 8×10 publicity shots, all signed and inscribed in ink, and Sig Bernstein appeared at my shoulder to narrate his treasures.

'Harlow never signed,' he yapped. 'If you see one, it's a fake – signed by her mother. Except for this one. Rare as hen's teeth. That's why it's priced at a grand, which is cheap, by the way. And Marlon Brando. He's rare – never liked signing. And that, right there, is the best Mansfield you'll ever see.'

Jayne Mansfield was shown beaming in an exceedingly low-cut dress that barely contained her enormous breasts. Her mouth was shaped into a big O.

'Oh my,' sighed Dad, as if Jayne Mansfield might be personally inviting him to stick a cucumber in her bottom. 'You know, Doobs, she was decapitated in a car accident?'

'I didn't know,' I said, struggling with that image.

'Yeah, and you won't see another like it,' said the old man. 'You get a lot of secretarial Mansfields. Most dealers can't tell the difference.'

'But *you* can, Sig,' said Dad. 'Haha. You've got a good eye.'

'I'll tell you a story,' growled Bernstein. 'As a kid I worked in the fan mail offices. The studios paid me forty cents an hour. I got so darn good at Bogart's signature I could write his name better than he could.'

'What, you mean you actually *signed* Humphrey Bogart's photographs on his behalf?' my father asked, excitedly.

'All day long. We did the five by sevens. Any five by sevens you ever see from the forties are secretarially signed. Betty Grable in red ink – that's a secretarial. Clark Gable in green – secretarial. The studios had a big operation going.'

Sig chuckled horribly to himself. Dad lightly punched the dealer on the shoulder and spread him a smile.

'But we just bought a Betty Grable five by seven,' I said.

'Oh, yes, Doobs. You'd better show Sig.'

I withdrew the photo from the paper bag, and the American snatched it and narrowed his blue eyes.

'Red ink. Like I said: secretarial.'

'Gosh,' said Dad.

'You'd better get yourselves a refund, kids.'

In the space of two seconds, the meaning of that photo had drained away completely. There hadn't been any link with Betty Grable. I'd been duped.

'Amazing,' said Dad, seeming impressed by the devastating news. 'Doobs, why don't you show Sig the rest of your collection.'

I withdrew my photo album sheepishly from my bag, and the old American was energized. He grabbed it, held it against his chest and flicked through rapidly.

'You'll find Laurence Olivier's daughter signed that one for him,' Sig announced, smiling nastily. 'And that Clint Eastwood is secretarial. Never signs his full name. Lucille Ball, Kirk Douglas – same thing. Secretarial.'

'What a shame. He's been writing to them all,' explained Dad. 'How awful.' Dad reached across to stoke my cheek, but I pulled away. 'It never even crossed my mind these actors had people signing for them.'

'That Neil Armstrong,' snarled Bernstein, 'is definitely not signed by him. It's an Autopen.'

'A what?' I shrieked.

The old man was laying into some of my favourites now. I wasn't going to take this lying down.

'A machine that signs autographs, kid. You write out your signature on a template, and the machine reproduces it over and over. JFK had one. Pretty much every letter he wrote was signed by machine. Ronald Reagan, the same. And all the astronauts. Ninety-nine per cent of Armstrong's are Autopen.'

'Oh,' I said, crestfallen. 'I can't believe these are all fake.'

'Autographs are a minefield, kid,' said Bernstein, pummelling my album into my chest and smiling cruelly. 'Oh, and by the way, that Sinatra is printed.'

'What? Is it really?' asked Dad, patting his face with his hand, offering his most shocked expression.

'Printed,' said Bernstein, slowly walking away from us down the aisle, before turning around to add, 'Frank don't like to sign.' The old man greeted a few dealers as he passed them, with the tiniest nod of his head.

'Well, interesting,' said Dad when we were alone again. 'Disappointing but interesting.'

'I don't believe the Sinatra's a print,' I said. 'He's wrong about that one.'

'Oh, Doobs, I think Sig knows what he's talking about. Come on. Let's take the Betty Grable back.'

Dad never tired of telling people about Bernstein's Harlow and his stunning Mansfield and how he used to sign Bogart's photographs in the film studios. He told people about my secretarial Clint Eastwood and my printed Sinatra and what an expert Sig was.

'It's all very mean,' he said. 'It seems these stars send out photos that are fakes. Poor Doobs.'

'I told you,' said Adam Brichto. 'Fake smile equals fake signature.'

'Not all of them,' I snarled. 'Some are real, like my Lauren Bacall and Debbie Reynolds.'

'Come on, forget it,' said Adam. 'Let's play darts.'

'And that's another thing,' I said. 'I think we should stop doing . . . that.'

Adam B protested, but in my new fallen universe I'd found respect for the truth and wanted to lay it on him.

'We're just pretending we like darts,' I said. 'It's all lies. Like Dad's lying to Mum. None of those women are actually enjoying themselves. Who on earth would enjoy a triple penetration? It's all fake.'

'Yeah, but who cares?' said Adam. 'We're enjoying it.'

I was troubled by the things Sig Bernstein said about my collection and felt compelled to now separate out the secretarials from the real ones. I needed to sever my connections. I couldn't believe how stupid I had been. Kirk Douglas hadn't been easy at all; he'd been a fraud. And what about my favourite? What about Sinatra? I examined that photo again carefully, and there was no denying that Sig was right. The handwriting indented the photo, but it wasn't made with a pen; it was machine-pressed into the picture with a silver varnish. It was easy to see now. I wished it was otherwise, but no. There was no Kirk Douglas and me. And there was no Frank Sinatra and me. The party was over.

Or was it? Something inside me was struggling with the new reality. I realized, suddenly, that I wanted the feeling back, that feeling of a personal connection with Frank Sinatra. Why should I give it up so easily? So, when I heard Dad arriving through the front door, I hastily grabbed one of my own silver pens, put a dot of ink at the end of Sinatra's name, then quickly smudged it. There. I ran downstairs to greet my father, waving the photo.

'Sig was wrong!' I announced. 'This Sinatra *is* signed in ink. Look, I smudged it, so it has to be real.'

Dad lifted his glasses and screwed his eyes up like Mr Magoo, then ran them up and down the photo a few times.

'Well, I never, Doobs,' he said. 'It is smudged.'

'Told you it was real,' I said.

'Which reminds me,' said Dad, fumbling with his briefcase. 'I've got a magazine for you. Sig sent it to my office.'

'A magazine?'

'It's for an autograph club.'

'Oh, that kind of magazine.'

Dad handed me a small blue booklet that had a signed photograph of Walt Disney on the front cover. The magazine was called *The Inkwell* and was produced by a company called the Worldwide Autograph Collectors' Club. I turned the cover and found a handwritten message in block capitals, to me: 'GOOD LUCK, KID. IT'S A MINEFIELD. SIG.'

'Very nice of him,' said Dad, smiling. 'And now you can get in touch with other collectors.'

'Wow,' I said, flicking through. I could see a long signature study on Walt Disney, an article on the best and worst in-person signers, plus an article entitled 'Why Collect Anything?'

'This has it all!' I shouted. It's even got celebrity addresses. Home addresses, not PO Boxes! Look!'

Dad smiled but seemed more interested in the ceiling in the next room.

'Dad?'

'Oh, Doobs,' he said, 'two of the lights have gone in the lounge. I must go and get some spare bulbs from the garage.'

CLINT EASTWOOD

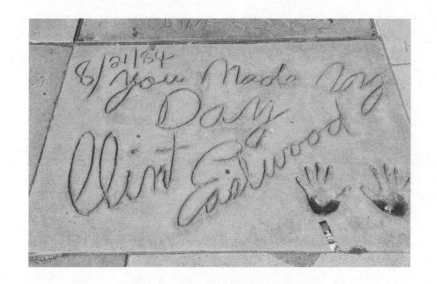

It takes tremendous discipline to control
the influence, the power you have
over other people's lives.

Clint Eastwood

In the summer of 1965, my father, Adrian Andrusier, led one of the first Jewish youth group tours of Israel. He and the other pioneers picked lemons with kibbutzniks, drank Marmara tea with Bedouins, watched the sun setting over the Negev Desert. Adrian was knocked sideways by the burgeoning new state where Jews were self-reliant and self-determined after millennia of persecution. To Adrian, the faces around him were etched with familiar Jewish pain; even the shiftiest taxi drivers passed for long-lost brothers. It was also a welcome break from the Tottenham council flat he shared with his mother and grandmother, where he slept in the lounge and the toilet was outside.

He returned home determined to begin a new life in the Promised Land. He sat down his newly widowed mother to break the news.

'You go, darling,' she said, 'and I'll put my head in the oven.'

He stayed.

It was around this time that Adrian met my mother. One of their first dates was a picnic. To Anna's dismay, Adrian brought along his mother – a talkative, self-centred woman with long red fingernails who kept grabbing her arm and calling her "darling". She couldn't understand why Adrian had allowed her to join.

'I couldn't very well leave her at home,' Adrian explained. 'She's all alone.'

Anna had her doubts, but her grandmother advised her that a man who was good to his mother would be good to his wife, so she put the doubts to the back of her mind.

Adrian began a career in insurance, married Anna and loyally supported his mother for the four remaining decades of her long life. Instead of emigrating, he focused on creating a secure future in England and rising up out of poverty. He found other ways to maintain his links to the country he loved. He expanded his collection of destroyed synagogues to include ephemera relating to hotels in pre-1948 Palestine: beer mats, promotional leaflets and souvenir postcards. And when he wasn't playing Big Bopper in the Volvo, he put on his favourite cassette, *The Story of Israel*, narrated by Robert Wagner's butler from *Hart to Hart*. The bit he liked best was when the nations gave their decisions at the UN General Assembly:

'Iran: *No*. Iraq: *No*. Lebanon: *No*.'

'You see,' Dad interjected, 'how all the Arab countries said no?'

When the creation of the Jewish state was finally announced, and violins sprang into action, he twitched with emotion. His eyes welled up and so did mine. It was all very moving, except I wasn't sure what we were so emotional about. I'd never even been to Israel. We normally went to the Algarve.

Adrian's main connection to the Holy Land came as something of a curveball. One day, some old pioneer friends, who'd remained in England and sacrificed the same dreams, invited him to an evening of Israeli folk dancing and general nostalgia about that 1965 trip. They talked about the old days on the kibbutz, the cleaning out of the chicken coops, the skits performed by the campfire, and they danced into the night. The evening made Adrian feel "free" and "connected" and "alive", and from 1983 onwards the group of old comrades expressed their love of Israel regularly on Thursday nights in a dingy Marylebone basement. They sweated, they twirled, they brushed hands – into the middle, then out again – while a bearded solicitor announced the songs over a microphone in heavily Scots-accented Hebrew. Accountancy, insurance, children and spouses were all left firmly at the door.

Most of my childhood was subject to the gravitational pull of these Thursday nights. Nothing short of a Beatles reunion would have convinced my father to miss a week. If, God forbid, some immovable object came in the way, say a school parents' evening, he would surrender so resentfully that we'd all feel guilty for weeks. It wasn't that we begrudged him his exercise, per se, just that the extent of his enjoyment was a little off.

'Dancing tonight!' he breezed on Thursday mornings, on the car journey to school.

'Actually, for me it's homework and piano practice.'

He wasn't listening. Because on Thursday nights, for Adrian, the rest of the world stopped dead.

Or, rather, on Thursdays, the world became one big spinning circle-dance.

If our weeks orbited around the formidable magnetic influence of Thursday nights, the month of August contained within it the 34-tonne superconducting neodymium magnet of our year. Because, every August, that same Scottish solicitor organized a six-day residential Israeli folk dance camp in Hertfordshire, and there was precisely zero chance of us Andrusiers missing it. Mum staged her futile protests each year. It wasn't fair to march us off to a camp against our will; none of us enjoyed the false merriment or the hype or the cornucopia of inadequate weirdos that awaited us at Hatfield Polytechnic. Oh, and none of us liked folk dancing.

'But *I* love it!' said Dad. '*I* want us to go. I want us to be together! Please, Lo-lo! I sit in the office all year round. It's the one thing I look forward to.'

The arguments always ended the same way: with the four of us traipsing up the A1 in the Volvo, my mother, my sister and I exchanging meaningful glances, swapping psychic messages of support.

§

It was August '87, the year Terry Waite got captured in Beirut. He'd carried on his shoulders Britain's historic involvement in the Middle East, and bravely headed to Lebanon to try to cool down some hot, fundamentalist tempers there. The cooling did not occur. Islamic Jihad marched him off the street at gunpoint. When Waite disappeared, the whole nation held its breath. Surely, he hadn't been taken hostage by the very terrorists he'd gone to negotiate with? Where was the fairness in that? Plus, I had an additional burden to bear – it had never even crossed my mind to write to him for an autograph.

That August, my family was interned, as usual, at Hatfield Polytechnic. The world's greatest talents in Israeli choreography showed up to delight and molest their fans. There was a dark-skinned yogi with capped teeth named Shlomiko, who could play two recorders simultaneously with his nose, a wolf-whistling Six Day War veteran named Yitzchak Golan who grew aubergines near Tel Aviv, and a small moustachioed man with a very tight bottom by the name of Mendel Mendel. In the early morn, a hundred Israeli folk dance enthusiasts from around the world, in spandex and sweatbands, stretched calves and love-of-Israel muscles. That year, there was a new contingent of late teens from the Soviet Union who'd only just discovered their Jewish heritage and been shipped over by an organization called the Joint. Someone at that organization had the brilliant idea of teaching these misplaced Jews Israeli folk dancing in Hatfield so they could export the dances back to the Eastern Bloc and teach other confused Jews how to become more Jewish.

As usual, Adrian planned his comedy skits well in advance. He talked them up for weeks, performed sections to his elderly mother at weekends. This year, he'd be playing a short-sighted rabbi performing a circumcision. He'd be staging a *This is Your Life, Shlomiko* show. And there'd be a rock 'n' roll quiz hosted by him, in character as Pinchas Blackburn.

'Why do you always have to be centre of attention?' challenged Mum as we lurched the Volvo onto the campus. 'It has to be about making people look at you.'

'Oh, Anna. I like entertaining,' he retorted. 'I'm one of the *machers*. If I don't do anything, people will be disappointed.'

'My God, why did I agree to come?' asked Mum, suddenly frantic, turning to us children in the back for answers. 'The greasy teachers and the blaring music, the recorders up the nose, the false merriment. It's always the same.'

'Well, because *I* love it,' exclaimed Dad. 'I love the dancing and I love the atmosphere. It makes me feel free.'

Mum turned to stare pleadingly at me and my sister, as if we were prison guards who might remove her handcuffs for good behaviour. I remembered poor, disappeared Terry Waite. I wondered what Terry would give right now to be arriving at Hatfield Polytechnic for six days of circle dancing. And what Mum would give to be locked up in a basement in Beirut.

As soon as the dancing and the blaring music got going, Adrian leapt in and left his family on the sidelines. He occasionally remembered we existed and beckoned us to join, but he was lithe and his hands slippery, and you soon lost him in the crowd. You saw him doing couple dances with young Ukrainian girls, locking eyes and rearranging the girls with stylized hand gestures. Mum would shake her head. Sometimes, the better dancers formed an extra circle in the middle. They whooped and jumped about, and you saw a blur of curly hair and knew your insurance salesman father was right in there, embedded with the biggest nuts.

While Adrian was placed in the advanced class, Mum was stuck in the intermediates. She sat at the side refusing to dance, with her hands on her ears to block out the astonishing volume of folk flute streaming through the speakers, akin to James Galway playing directly into your ear canal. I'd heard how hostages went into a state of denial at the start of their ordeals, the enormity of their situation too great to contemplate.

My sister coped with captivity by burying her head in nineteenth-century literature, while I spent the days consulting copies of *The Inkwell* and deciding which celebrities to write to. Each issue featured thirty or forty addresses to try. I brought along reams of paper and handwrote letter after letter, straining to reach out to the world beyond the barbed wire of Hatfield. Armed with expert advice from this publication, I'd already got autographs that had previously eluded me. It really had been a question of addresses. You wanted to avoid PO Boxes and PR agencies, it turned out, where the secretaries either ignored your letters or signed the autographs themselves. For example, it was a waste of time writing to Paul McCartney at MPL Communications in Soho because it never actually got to him. Try writing to his home address in Leigh-on-Sea five or six times and you got an authentic signed photograph with 'To Adam, all the best, Paul McCartney' written in blue ink.

The magazine also published the names and addresses of other collectors, along with their areas of interest. It fascinated me to see what my kindred spirits around the globe were looking for. Hockey stars, cowgirls, Nobel Prize winners, child actors. It was endless. Some wanted signed photos, others wanted cancelled cheques, some were only interested in plain signatures. Once my name got printed in there, I received dozens of letters from other collectors who wanted to trade signatures and celebrity addresses. Mostly, though, they wanted to trade success stories about their own collections and taunt me with photocopies of the things they would never sell, sometimes even sending photographs of themselves holding their prize possessions.

One particularly friendly person was Darren Pendle from Leicester. He was seventeen. He told me that if you sent 8×10 photographs to the celebrities and enclosed stamped-addressed envelopes, you had a better chance of a response. He gave me the phone number of a photograph dealer in Bushey by the name of Peter Oxtonby. I phoned up, and Oxtonby obliged with his catalogue, which was a thick sheaf of photocopied pages, each rammed with thumbnail images of the photos he had available at £1.50 each. The last page was an order form, which you sent back with a cheque. When my grandparents went on holiday to Hawaii, I had them bring back several sheets of stamps so I could make up stamped-addressed envelopes for the Americans, then I sent out 8×10s to Jack Nicholson, Robert Redford, Dustin Hoffman and the rest. The results were pleasing, and some celebrities, like James Stewart, didn't even mind you sending them three or four different poses to sign. Which gave me duplicates to trade with the other collectors . . .

My other pen pals included Yogesh Gupta, a middle-aged eye surgeon at the Newcastle Royal Victoria Infirmary looking for autographs of Ray Charles, Stevie Wonder and Helen Keller. And Connor Thomas III, who lived with a parrot in a remote region of northern Canada and collected the autographs of surviving cast members of *The Wizard of Oz*. The survivors were all Munchkins. Connor had personally located and befriended numerous of these ancient actors in retirement homes in California and regularly sent me images of himself sitting next to tiny shrivelled individuals – him smiling, them not so much.

Lunch at the camp was served in the college dining hall, termed the "prison canteen" by Mum. Adrian bounded in, drenched with sweat after a morning of dancing, a born-again gleam in his eye.

'You look exhausted,' said Mum.

'I'm not. I feel good.' Adrian flexed his arms to demonstrate just how good. 'Now, Lo-lo, are we going to do *our* sketch this evening?'

'What sketch is that?' asked my sister.

'You'll have to wait and see!' glistened Dad.

'I'm not doing it,' said Mum, placing her knife and fork across her plate. 'I'm not interested in all this escapism. And I don't want to be controlled.'

I'd heard about an American hostage who'd been blind-folded for months at a time; he sustained himself through the power of prayer alone.

'Let's do it on the last night, then,' reasoned Dad. 'Tonight, I'll do *This is Your Life, Shlomiko*. It's bound to be a success. Now, when will you do your song, childries? I've asked Sterling to play the guitar for you, like last year.'

Ruth and I exchanged urgent glances.

'Er, not this year,' I said. 'I don't want people looking at me.'

I was feeling strong; a long way off from breaking, my spirit bolstered by the network of pen pals I'd grown around me, famous and civilian alike. It drifted into mind that I owed Katharine Hepburn a letter.

Yitzchak Golan joined us abruptly at our table, enshroud-ing us in a sweet-smelling cloud of sweat. He sucked in his potbelly and slid onto the wooden bench, then stared at us as if we were museum exhibits.

'You know, Ad-ree-an, I was shot four times,' he yelled.

Yitzchak's voice was fixed at yelling volume as usual. He delivered his devastating news with great cheer, but I noticed a dullness in his eyes, as if the cheer came at some internal cost. He stroked and shaped his rainforest of a moustache with both hands.

'What do you think about it?'

'Shot, Yitzchak?' asked Adrian, wide-eyed. 'You weren't!'

'Here. Here. Here,' shouted Golan, pointing to his elbow, thigh and shoulder in turn. 'And once here.'

He pointed to his forehead, above and to the left of one eye, where there was a small dent. He flashed a grin but there was that sad glint again. He was fidgety now. He turned away, distracted by something.

'Oh my God,' said Adrian. 'That's unbelievable! But how incredible that you survived!'

'I killed who did it, don't worry. Three Arabs, Ad-ree-an. I shot them. Then I crawl for three kilometres in the desert.'

'You crawled? Impossible!'

'No water. Agony. But I'm strong. I tell myself: the most important thing is never give up.'

Adrian patted Golan on the shoulder and the giant responded by grabbing my father's hand and bending the fingers so far back that he winced in pain. Then the man mountain reached under the table and squeezed *my* thigh till I yelped. He did all this while narrowing his eyes flirtatiously at my sister.

'You're hurting him,' exclaimed Mum.

'Hurting?' asked Golan, squeezing my other leg now with his fist of steel. 'What is mean? It's not hurt.'

Then he sprang to his feet and started massaging Dad's shoulders.

'Ow! Ow!' laughed Adrian. 'Yitzchak, that's painful!'

'I'm *relax* you,' said Golan. 'Is important to relax.'

'Stop, Yitzchak! Come on. Ouch! Look, I tell you what. I've got a sketch for us to do.'

That did the trick. The dance teacher loosened his grip and ran after Adrian into the kitchens. Minutes later, out they came, my father wearing a Hassidic beard, thick glasses and a bloodied apron, Golan cradling one of my sister's old dolls which had a long balloon attached to its crotch. Adrian fumbled his way through the room, leaning on chairs, pretending to be blind. The international crowd exploded into peals of laughter at the impromptu circumcision.

When the skit was over and Adrian was sitting back down, a slight Frenchman, Roger, approached our table to say that this had been one of the funniest things he had ever seen. Roger, who was employed by the French government to think up disaster scenarios, was a morose individual with a permanent cold that caused him to return periodically to his room to steam. 'Senk you, Adrien,' he bleated, unsmilingly. 'Really. Senk you.' Then he said to my mother, 'It must be truly great to be married to this man.'

The last night of the camp traditionally included the funniest performance pieces. And so, on the main stage of Hatfield Polytechnic's great hall, Mum now perched on Adrian's knee pretending to be a ventriloquist's dummy, a Pinocchio nose attached to her face, while Adrian – wearing a false Hassidic beard – pretended to be her ventriloquist.

'Good evening, ladies and gentlemen,' shouted my father's voice.

My mother's mouth opened and closed.

'Are you having a lovely time?'

Again, Mum's jaw was in sync.

The audience cried out 'Yeeees!'

'What do you call a woman who knows where her husband is all the time?' asked Adrian through Mum's mouth.

The assembled dance fanatics fell about laughing, while my sister and I searched each other's faces for signs of hope.

'A widow.'

I wondered if I should let off a smoke bomb and storm the stage, SAS-style. We could cause a distraction and drag my mother off. But then I noticed the spiteful look on her face. She wasn't *empathizing* at all. With her silently yacking jaw she was, in fact, ridiculing her captor and all he stood for, while simultaneously showing up her audience for the imbeciles they were. This wasn't Butlins; this was avant-garde theatre.

When the performance ended, Yitzchak Golan lifted my father up onto his shoulders and paraded him around the hall, shouting, 'Adree-an, Adree-an, Adree-an.' Mendel Mendel joined in, jogging behind like an overly conspicuous Mossad agent. Deafening music once again blared through the speakers in the polytechnic's main hall, an oompah-oompah accordion with a clarinet screeching over the top, and the last-night party began in earnest. A huge circle of people was spinning around the room, performing a medley of routines taught during the week. People were emotional. Really emotional. Having live breakdowns, in fact. What they'd created together here in Hatfield in Technicolor was now drawing to a close; they would soon be returning to their black-and-white existences around the globe. Everywhere you looked people were hugging, exchanging phone numbers, squeezing out the last bit of group love.

'It's none of it real,' sniffed Mum, discarding her Pinocchio nose.

There was very little conversation on the car journey home. A sort of happy tiredness pervaded the Volvo as Dad drove us back towards safety. The grey breeze blocks of Hatfield

Polytechnic receded into the distance for another year. Now it was just a question of opening the post on the porch floor. I spooled through the list of people I'd written to over the previous few weeks. Perhaps Schulz had finally deigned to draw me a Snoopy, now that I was six years old with a broken leg?

'I've been awake all night, but I feel just fine,' Dad said, addressing no one in particular as we approached Apex Corner. 'I think I'll go dancing tonight. Do you want to come?'

A wave of shock swept through the car.

'Tonight? Is that some kind of joke?'

'It's not a joke, Lo-lo. A group of us are meeting in Covent Garden for dinner, then going back to Maurice's for dancing. It'll be fun. We should all go!'

'Please, no,' said Ruth.

'We can't,' I said.

'You've been awake all night, Adrian,' tried Mum. 'We've been dancing for six days solid. The children are exhausted – they were up till midnight last night. Look at the bags under their eyes! Don't you know when enough is enough?'

'I want us to go!'

No one spoke after that. Mum massaged her temples, while my sister and I stared out of the window. We were being driven away from captivity by our captor. Who had we been kidding?

We pulled into our driveway in Pinner, and I jumped out of the car to see what treasures had arrived. Dad opened the front door, and a big pile of envelopes was sitting there. I rummaged through, quickly finding an exciting one: Clint

Eastwood's home address stamped in blue on the back. I'd only ever got secretarial autographs, but *The Inkwell* had given me his home address in Carmel, and I'd sent three 8×10s. I revealed the signed photos one by one to Dad, each signed by Clint himself with a scrawl – nothing like all the legible secretarials, and way more stylish than the careful, babyish signature traced in concrete at Grauman's Chinese Theatre. One of the photos was a reproduction of the poster for *Escape from Alcatraz* and showed Eastwood's face appearing through a chink at the end of a tunnel, his sharpened spoon in hand. Clint had, pleasingly, placed his signature in black pen to a very light portion. The condition was excellent due to the envelope stiffeners I'd used.

'Look, Dad. An authentic Clint Eastwood.'

'Now, are you sure that's his actual signature?' asked Dad. 'You know what Sig said.'

'It's real, Dad! I've seen a signature study in *The Inkwell*. It's got the long "C" and the sharp angle between "Clint" and "Eastwood". It's the real thing!'

'Very good, Doobs. And *Escape from Alcatraz* is a great film. You do know it's not true, though, don't you?'

'What do you mean? What's not true?'

'Well, the story's not true. Because in real life no one ever actually escaped. The security was too good. The ones that got out were either shot or drowned. Very strong currents in the sea.'

I squared up for a fight, but Dad's smile was too earnest. It's not about the actual *escape*, silly, I should have said. The escape's neither here nor there. It's about a bid for freedom! It's about the human capacity for hope! It's about man's ineluctable belief in his own destiny! But I was twelve years old. So, instead, I tried Mum's trick. I opened and closed my mouth soundlessly, wiggled my head sarcastically from side to side and hoped for the best.

Terry Waite was released in November 1991 after 1,763 days of captivity, much of that time spent in solitary confinement. In his memoirs he described how he sustained himself with hope. He recalled saying inwardly to his captors, 'You have the power to break my body and bend my mind, but my soul is not yours to possess.'

LIZ TAYLOR

Big girls need big diamonds.

Elizabeth Taylor

The *Monty Python* sketch I liked when I was thirteen was the one where Michael Palin plays a milkman. He whistles as he sets down bottles on the doorstep of a terraced house. The door opens, and he looks up to see a bare-footed housewife towering above him. She has a humungous cleavage and is wearing a see-through negligee. Shimmering violins start up – Wagner. Under that negligee she's completely naked. You can see it when you pause the Betamax. The woman beckons the milkman inside, and he nervously follows up the carpeted staircase, licking his lips. The music swells, the violins soar. She turns to tousle her hair and displays that naked buttock. Then she opens an upstairs door for the milkman, and in he goes. But she doesn't follow. Instead, she slams the door behind him and locks it from the outside. The music stops. Palin looks around, startled, to find he's in a room full of other milkmen, all sporting beards of varying lengths. The others look up, then lower their eyes again and sigh. In the corner is a skeleton wearing a milkman's hat.

§

Our parties were held at Çağlayan Turkish restaurant in Hendon. For my parents' twentieth wedding anniversary, Adrian booked out half the place. This, despite Anna's protestations. She said an anniversary should be something private, something between two people and not for public consumption. She didn't fancy being "paraded around" and "stared at". But Adrian insisted it would be fun to celebrate the big day with friends, and at Çağlayan you could even have dancing.

He arrived at the restaurant an hour early and plastered the walls with doctored images of himself and Anna. Adrian marrying Elizabeth Taylor, Anna marrying JFK, the two of them as Elizabeth and Philip at the coronation. And one photo showing Mum and Dad's actual wedding. Mum is twenty-two, as stunning as Audrey Hepburn, with sad, secretive eyes. Dad stands at her elbow, looking more like a publicist than a husband. He waves triumphantly at the camera.

When the friends arrived, Adrian made a speech about how his wedding day seemed just like yesterday. He said Anna was a fabulous cook and the best wife he could have hoped for, even if she didn't enjoy Israeli dancing. That made the crowd laugh. He added a bit about her being a talented sculptress, and how modest she was about those talents, which made the guests go all doe-eyed and stare at Mum just the way she'd feared they might. I thought of the sculptures displayed around our house. Naked bodies in telling poses, reaching out, straining for things beyond their grasp. Whenever Mum showed her sculptures to Dad, he stared for a while then said, 'So, what's that supposed to be, then?'

After the speech, Adrian asked the manager to put on his Israeli folk dance cassette. The friends formed a wonky circle down the centre of the restaurant and did folk dances while the strangers at the other tables looked on, quietly sipping their drinks, perhaps wondering if this was what all the Jews did on Saturday evenings. Adrian took hundreds of photos while Anna put on her bravest face. She laughed and Israeli-danced and patted her chest at friends' jokes, but it was clear she was suffering. She'd wanted a quiet evening at home with her husband. She'd said that was what she wanted.

For me, the best bit at Çağlayan was dessert, served from a table-clothed trolley on wheels. Crème brûlée, crème caramel, fruit salad and Sultan's cake.

'Ooh, such a handsome boy,' pronounced the waiter with no neck, his hand slipping as he poured extra double cream onto my cake. 'Soon, you break all the girls' hearts.'

'Yeah . . . Any second now.'

'You'll see, you'll see!' laughed the waiter, jabbing a finger.

'Maybe don't break any hearts?' suggested my fifteen-year-old sister, mournfully turning a chunk of pineapple around her bowl.

'Don't worry, Ruthie,' I said. 'I won't, really.'

I pictured hearts pumping with blood in a long, neat line; someone offering a sledgehammer and me politely declining.

Lately, my parents' friends had been on a similar trip to this waiter. They had me all decided. They told me I was poised to get "the pick of the bunch", "make all the girls cry" and cause "havoc" for my parents. 'Still playing the piano?' they'd taunt. 'You'll have other things on your mind, soon.' I nodded and humoured them, but it was all patently nonsense. The pick of which bunch? Break whose heart? If these people didn't have names and numbers, I wasn't buying it.

It was my bar mitzvah that sounded the starting pistol on all this erotic speculation. I put in a soprano performance worthy of Kiri Te Kanawa, yet they still asked me afterwards how it felt to be a man. 'Great,' I squeaked. 'Loving every minute.' Thank God, at thirteen and a half, my voice was now finally breaking. Not cracking in half like some of the boys, more casually bending. I tested it each day on the piano;

down a semitone per week. And I was changing shape, too – fattening and lengthening in rotation. There was no denying that the whole of me was going somewhere; it just wasn't clear where. If I was lucky, sure, I'd end up in the good pile, feasting my eyes on the pick of the bunch. But it could go the other way. I could become one of those boys with gangly faces, infected spots and overbites, eyes roving around like a murderer. For every boy breaking a girl's heart there had to be five or six putting her off her lunch.

In those days, I spent a lot of time imagining myself annihilating the hearts of pretty girls. I'd kissed two already, but only one was a French kiss. She probed my mouth like a dentist and asked me to open wider. I hadn't got near any breasts yet, and anyway wouldn't have known what to do with one. But that didn't stop me thinking about them. I also meditated, deeply, on what exactly was going on with my manhood, which was not as much as I'd have liked – analogous to the semitone per week. The possibility of getting a girl involved with that part of my anatomy seemed every bit as remote as getting this cross-eyed waiter with the double cream acquainted with the Theory of Relativity.

Recently, my father had been getting in on the act, too; never one to be upstaged. He'd twice begun a tutorial about *Lady Chatterley's Lover*, and Lawrence's use of the word "cunt" before I managed to shut it down. He also decided that now I was thirteen it was time to turn the volume of Marvin Gaye right down and share with me everything he knew about the Final Solution. He delivered this in a course of lectures in the Volvo on Thursday mornings in a low, excitable tone. He began with the Nazis' early methods of killing Jews. He spoke of euthanasia, of ambulances with exhaust pipes fed back in, then he moved on to the *Einsatz-gruppen*. He finished up by describing, with some aplomb, the mass exterminations at Treblinka and Auschwitz.

'Have a great day, Doobs!' he called out of the Volvo window. 'Won't see you tonight because of dancing.'

I spent my days in circular consideration of gassings and girls, mass graves and my burgeoning masculinity. I thought about Mum's grandparents – how they'd been actually murdered by the Nazis for no good reason, probably with gas, and how no one knew exactly where and when they'd died. And I got curious about Dad's great interest in the Holocaust, when his own side of the family had been in England during the war, dodging conscription.

§

Around this time, Adrian decided I was ready for the world of auctions. He brought home a catalogue for a London auction house that was holding an "Entertainment sale". When he handed it over, I saw he'd already heavily thumbed it and added asterisks, as if there were things here we might actually buy. He'd marked lots that included Bill Haley or Buddy Holly or Danny Kaye or Elizabeth Taylor, and he double underlined or circled those names as if they were top of our hit list. I went through and added asterisks of my own. Some of the better items were in single lots, but many lots seemed to consist of whole collections. One description read:

> Lot 81: Ten autograph albums featuring
> more than five hundred signatures including
> Judy Garland, Boris Karloff, Elizabeth Taylor
> and others.   £100–150

Adrian had underlined 'Garland' and 'Taylor', and put a double circle around 'and others'.

'Five hundred signatures!' I exclaimed. 'But they've only listed three.'

'Exactly. There must be other interesting names in there. We should go and take a look.'

The viewing was held just before the sale, and they had 1940s music playing. The lots were stored in tall glass cases, and businessmen sat browsing at a central group of desks. Auction house assistants unlocked the cases and fetched the precious lots for you while you waited. We sat down and asked for lot 81, then gasped as we turned the pages of the albums, all lovingly filled with signatures. Each autograph bore witness to a tiny moment some forty years earlier – captured it forever on the page. I was mesmerized by how each famous person had their own unique way of signing their name that no one else could reproduce; the curly, the angular, the decorative, the illegible. I thought about my own signature, how whenever I practised it in my school rough book it felt like my way of proving I existed, proving I was really me.

'Ooh, she died young,' said Adrian, shaking his head sadly when we got to Judy Garland's flowery signature. 'And look, there's Elizabeth Taylor. She was lovely. She's put the date too, look: 1946. Can't have been much more than your age, back then.'

I'd written to Taylor a few times, but all you ever got was a photo of her with a later-life mop of hair, signed sloppily by her secretary, 'All the best, Elizabeth Taylor'. But this signature in the autograph album was early and childlike and definitely in Taylor's own hand. There was still so much to be decided in her life in 1946. *Cleopatra* hadn't happened. Her heart hadn't yet been broken by Richard Burton or any of the others. I stared at it with desirous eyes; I wanted to own that signature, seal it up in my collection. I remembered, now, that Darren Pendle was looking for an early Taylor, and she was on Yogesh Gupta's "want list" too. They wouldn't get this one, though; this was mine. But there was so much more to come in these albums! We spotted Laurel and Hardy, four Charlie Chaplins, a Marilyn, no fewer than six Sinatras, Cagney, Mansfield, Alfred Hitchcock with a little sketch, Walt Disney × 2. It went on and on. I made a long list around the edge of the catalogue.

'How can they not have noticed all these?' asked Adrian. 'It's bizarre. And how can the estimate be this low?'

'We have to buy it, Dad. Collectors in *The Inkwell* will pay two hundred US dollars for a vintage Sinatra, and there are six of them here! Walt Disney's worth five hundred dollars. And an early Liz Taylor has to be three hundred or more.'

'Let's see what happens,' said Adrian. 'You never know.'

We gave the lot back to the assistant and carried on flicking through the catalogue.

A familiar American voice boomed behind us.

'Don't worry, kids. You won't get a thing.'

It was Sig Bernstein, smiling mercilessly. A cloud of rotten breath settled over us.

'Sig! Fancy seeing you here!' said Adrian, turning to shake hands.

'I'm buying everything,' said Sig. 'Go home and get your tea, kids.'

Sig bought everything.

*

It wasn't long after that I saw an advert in the *Evening Standard* stating that the megastar Elizabeth Taylor would be personally appearing at Selfridges the following day at 5 p.m. to promote her new perfume, 'Passion'. I figured if I couldn't get her autograph in the post or at auction, this might be my only opportunity.

It wasn't the first time I'd gone out clasping the black book Adrian had bought me at Woolworths, with 'AUTO-GRAPHS' on the front in gold letters. On the advice of pen pals I'd begun turning up to theatres on opening nights, where you never knew who might attend. It turned out people like me were known as "in-person collectors" in the trade. The opening nights were exciting, but it was mostly small-fry celebrities. I got Ed Asner and Warren Mitchell and Judi Dench. Terry Wogan pretended not to see me, and Jonathan Miller said he didn't "do" autographs. Often, I had no idea who the famous people were, and had to follow the other collectors around to see what they did. Many of the collectors were older than my parents. I also made use of the paparazzi. If you saw them snapping a picture, it had to be someone famous. I got Robert Beatty that way, and Mary Martin and Edward Fox. And there was one pair of celebrities that showed up time and time again in their Rolls-Royce. 'Bloody Michael Winner and Fiona Fullerton,' grumbled the photographers, backing off in disgust.

On the day in question, I got out of school at 4 p.m. and legged it down Finchley Road. I took the Tube to Bond Street and got to Selfridges circa 4.45 p.m. In the perfume hall were huge photographs on the walls of Elizabeth Taylor in her prime, glistening with jewels alongside various husbands, and there were rows and rows of photographers. Throngs of fans waited expectantly, and I quickly realized there was no way I'd get close. Something made me think of the car park. She had to have arrived by car. Which meant she would be leaving the same way, once the appearance was over.

I found my way to the back of the shop and followed signs. It didn't take long to spot a black limousine with a man holding a huge camera standing next to it.

'Is this Liz Taylor's?' I gasped.

'Yeah, she's gone in,' muttered the photographer. 'Gonna catch her on the way out.'

Him and me both. I was the only fan there, and thirteen years old to boot. I figured I had Liz cornered. She'd have to sign. I trembled with excitement at the encounter ahead and dug in for the wait, my short autograph career passing before my eyes. The Thompson Twins, Big Daddy, Judi Dench; they were nothing compared to Liz Taylor!

Eventually, after a full half-hour that felt like an eternity, the door to the car park was flung open, and right before my eyes was Elizabeth Taylor. It was as if everything went into slow motion, as if she was appearing through a cloud of smoke. If it had been a *Monty Python* sketch, the Wagner would have started up around now. She had four body-guards marching on either side of her. She trained her violet eyes on me and smiled. Liz Taylor was looking right at me! Any second now, and I'd have her signature locked away in my book.

'Miss Taylor, can I please have your autograph?' I yelped.

And we had a moment together, Liz and I. We looked deep into each other's souls. I thought of the youthful sig-nature I'd passed my fingers over, days earlier. And, seeing my young face, I fancied Liz was thinking about her own hopes and dreams at my age, when there was still so much to be decided. The big camera flashed over and over.

But then something else happened. A deadness took hold of the actress's gaze. She switched off. She'd been through this a million times. We were not kindred spirits. I was thirteen, she was fifty. I was just another deranged fan. Besides, she had other things to attend to. A face lift? Dinner date with a future husband? The Wagner record scratched to a halt.

'Sorry,' said Liz Taylor. 'I can't.'

With that, she jumped into her car, and it screeched out of the car park. The photographer blew his nose and sloped off.

A part of me was bitterly disappointed, but another part oddly relieved. Relieved at what? I couldn't put my finger on it. It was like that moment when you dared yourself to jump into a freezing-cold swimming pool without testing the water, then at the last moment decided against it. Liz Taylor was out of my league, that was all. My desire had got the better of me. I suddenly remembered, for some reason, how that *Monty Python* sketch I liked ended. You saw those ageing milkmen trapped in a room, then it cut to a man sitting at a desk writing out a sentence and saying it aloud: 'The room is full of milkmen, some of whom are very old.'

§

At 10 p.m., at Çağlayan, the owner shushed the crowd to make a big announcement. He said that in honour of my parents' loyal patronage these past fifteen years, we would be getting a rare treat. Loud Turkish music came crashing in, involving a lot of bongo drums, and a woman in a white skirt and bra with silver tassels was suddenly let in. She wiggled through the crowd like a bemused calf at a cattle auction. She wasn't especially smiling. All the husbands clapped in time to the music and feasted their eyes on the boobs and smooth midriff that waggled by, each trying to catch the dancer's attention. The wives, meanwhile, lowered their gaze, inter-linked their fingers on the tables, seemed to be waiting for it to end.

The dancer had finger cymbals in each hand and clinked them whenever she wanted to dance with someone. The hus-bands loved being chosen. They glanced at their wives for permission, then jumped to their feet with unseemly speed and started wiggling their hefty frames from side to side, doing air finger cymbals at the now extremely bored-looking dancer, while the other husbands looked on jealously. When she'd had enough, the dancer thrust her boobs towards the man's face and waited for him to put a banknote right there in the middle, before moving on to someone else.

'Bet you're hoping she'll dance with you,' said Dad's ac-countant's wife, appearing at my side just as the belly dancer's bouncy flesh started careering down the central aisle.

'Dunno,' I said. 'Don't think I'm her type.'

It turned out I was. The belly dancer locked eyes with me and raised her eyebrows. I wasn't an accountant, I sup-posed, and I wasn't forty-four, so maybe I came as a welcome change? I was nervous. She narrowed her eyes, seemingly detecting my resistance. Still, before I knew it, she was clink-ing her finger cymbals right at me and twirling her boobs. I could see Adrian in the corner of my eye, teeing up his camera and grinning. I could see the other husbands glancing at their watches, their wives' eyes lighting up for the first time since the hors d'oeuvres.

The belly dancer gyrated in front of me, as if to say I was all hers and could do with her exactly as I wished.

The room is full of husbands, I thought. *Some of whom are very old.*

'Sorry,' I said, in my kindliest voice. 'I can't.'

GARBO

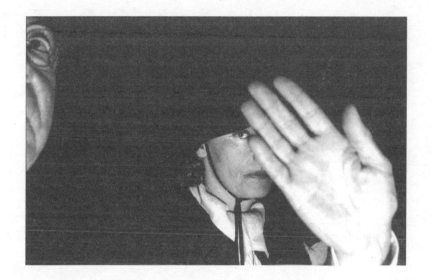

Anyone who has a continuous smile
on his face conceals a toughness
that is almost frightening.

Greta Garbo (née Gustafsson)

Mum's parents were Czech, which was why they rolled their r's, wore smart clothes and hummed classical music whenever the other was talking. My grandfather grew up out of poverty to become a successful businessman, buying and selling plastic goods. He did a lot of escaping: the Nazis in 1938, then the Russians in 1948. When he settled in England, he changed his name. He went from Schwartzmann to Sheldon in one fell swoop; opened a phone book and looked under 'S'.

My grandmother was plump but vain. She didn't laugh freely because she worried about wrinkles; when photographed, she always turned to display her profile. But, like Mum, you knew her brain was ticking away even when she was quiet, because of the way her face shifted at odd moments. If I asked, 'Penny for your thoughts,' my grandma's face relaxed into a big smile. Then she smacked my hand.

Lotka was seventeen when she married my grandfather. Professional black-and-white photos documented young, fresh-faced film stars staring into a wonderful future together. By contrast, the only photograph that existed of Grandpa Jožka's own parents sat on top of the television in a black frame, and showed simple, hard-working peasants with no idea of the grim fate awaiting them. Grandpa had tried to convince them to leave Czechoslovakia in 1938, but they thought he was exaggerating the danger. It was a mystery where and when they died, but most Czech Jews were sent to Theresienstadt concentration camp, then on to Auschwitz. We sometimes heard a story about Grandpa's brother, Aron, how he'd escaped from a train. But no one knew the details, and no one knew for sure. My mother sometimes said we should try to find him, and I had fantasies of locating him in the Eastern Bloc and bringing him to London for a huge, joyous reunion.

My grandfather, Jožka, was a man who knew how things should be done. If you asked him for advice, he gave it to you. If you didn't ask for advice, he gave it to you. While Adrian spoke in paragraphs that spiralled out of control, Jožka was succinct: 'What can you lose?', 'The question is this', 'Be careful'. If he was ill, he would shut himself in a room and say, 'I have a cold. No further bulletins will be issued.' Grandpa Jožka was the law. He was like a judge or a president, and good luck to anyone who disagreed with him. Being married to him had to be the toughest job in town, Mum said, because he was so damaged – because of what had happened to his parents. In the old days, Grandma Lotka apparently got so pent up and frustrated that she'd smash old jam jars in the garage to let off steam, or pretend to faint just to win an argument.

Grandpa Jožka often picked me up from school ('What time do I pick you?' he'd ask), then I'd go back to the house in Kingsbury and wait for Mum to collect me from there. Grandma made sure her husband worked hard for me on such occasions.

'Go and cut some apple for your grandson,' she barked.

'No sooner said than done,' replied Grandpa, backing out of the lounge like a sommelier.

'And bring some biscuits. Some *vanilkové rohlíčky*.'

My grandmother arranged a blanket over me and stroked my forehead.

'My grandson's wish is my command,' came Grandpa's voice.

While he toiled away in the kitchen, my grandmother and I watched old films on the sofa. *Meet Me in St Louis*, *The Wizard of Oz*, *Casablanca* and *Grand Hotel*, where Greta Garbo plays a lonely ballerina, bemoaning a floundering dancing career. She's so despondent, she wants to be left alone, but then she falls in love with the mysterious Baron. At the end, she leaves the hotel to start a new life with her lover; unbeknown to her, he's already dead.

'They sometimes said I resembled her when I was young,' my grandmother said.

'You still do, Grandma.'

'Ach, don't be ridiculous. Now I look like her great-aunt.'

'No. You look like her.'

'Your grandma was a good-looking girl when we were young,' concurred Grandpa Jožka, appearing with a crystal bowl of neatly cut-up, peeled apple. 'But with her upturned nose, no one believed she was Jewish. Isn't it true, *zlato*?'

My grandma pointed crossly to exactly where her husband should place the bowl, then shooed him away with a swipe of her hand.

§

There was no point in writing to Garbo. In autograph terms, she was basically dead. The only example I'd seen was in Sig Bernstein's folder, for £1,000. A big curly signature.

Brando, Sinatra, Newman – they all used secretaries, and rarely signed in person. But Garbo was a vanishing act. Sure, the autograph magazine published her New York address and we tried our luck, but it was useless. Even if you knew what she looked like, which no one did, you had precisely zero chance of her signing. It was something she'd decided not to do. No autographs. No exceptions. And no one knew why.

'She doesn't like the limelight,' Dad suggested, twisting the lens of his Kodak to catch a moody shot of Mum making meatloaf in the kitchen.

'So, how can I force her to sign?' I mused.

'I suppose if you threaten her?' suggested Dad.

'Adrian,' came Mum's voice.

'Or, I don't know. Maybe you could *trick* her into signing?'

'She's too clever,' I said. 'Sig Bernstein told me a story about her paying for shoes in a shop in New York. She signed a cheque in the name of Harriet Brown, which is an alias she uses. The shop staff recognized her and realized how valuable the handwriting was, so the boss didn't pay the cheque in – he kept it. A week later, he got an angry call from Garbo's assistant. "Why haven't you cashed the cheque? Can you do it right away?"'

'Amazing,' said Dad, trying to get an aerial shot of my pile of collector's albums on the living-room floor.

'I suppose,' said Mum, exiting the lounge in her apron, 'she got sick of studio bosses making her lose weight, and got tired of all the schmoozing and bamboozling. She'd had enough.'

Garbo was a festering sore for us autograph collectors; a problem that couldn't be solved. The mere mention of her name sent us into paroxysms of fidget and headshaking. Hers was the rarest living autograph, at a value of £100 for each letter of her name. I decided the best thing I could do was forget about it; force it to the back of my mind, just as I'd done with penile cancer and nuclear war.

Then, one day in the barber's waiting room, I got to page 4 of the *Sun*, to discover an article by a journalist who'd tracked Garbo down to a ski resort in Switzerland. He'd even chatted to her on a hotel sofa. 'I just want to be alone, darling,' she was quoted as saying, tugging on the reporter's arm.

When I got home, I put pen to paper, and wrote to that journalist care of the *Sun*. If he was on friendly terms with Garbo, couldn't he get her autograph for me? Her biggest fan. Her youngest. A fanatic. My grandmother was mistaken for her!

No reply. But I'd be heading to Switzerland soon enough, myself.

§

We went skiing with Mum's parents each year, and each year Grandma Lily got in a huff about her exclusion. The problem was she was an East Ender, and Mum's parents were Czech, so putting them together was like serving roast goose with a pile of greasy chips. The Czech grandparents bristled impatiently at the East Ender diatribes about shopping trips to Sainsbury's and special offers, while Lily made barbed comments about how "the other half lived", meaning my Czech grandparents' month-long holidays in Hawaii. 'Going away again?' she'd ask, when she saw them. 'Don't you get tired of all the travel?'

Also, since our traumatic tour of the South of France with Grandma Lily, whose French accent could crack a wine glass, Mum had vowed never to holiday with her again. It was hard enough seeing Lily every weekend in London. She talked literally non-stop and never listened. She made claustrophobic speeches about how we were her "little family" and no one else mattered, how blood was thicker than water, how we were all she thought about. Dad phoned her every night and held the phone at arm's length because the conversation was so unbearable; while Dad massaged his temples and tried to breathe, you'd hear Grandma Lily's voice jabbering away in the background.

Just Dad's luck that this particular year, three days before our departure, his mother had a freak accident and broke her leg.

'I feel awful leaving her alone in hospital,' he intoned in the Volvo, staring fearfully into the traffic. 'I'm all she's got. I should really stay home and keep her company.'

'Well, hang on a minute, Adrian,' said Mum. 'That would be a bit drastic. Don't forget, I've arranged for that woman, Sue, to spend the days with her. So, she's not going to be alone. And she seemed perfectly happy with that arrangement. In fact, she said we should go away and enjoy ourselves, and stop worrying. Those were her exact words.'

'She won't like the hospital food,' breathed Adrian, shaking his head and clasping his chin. 'She'll hate it. We'll have to make sure that Sue brings in plenty of extra things.'

'I've got it covered,' said Mum. 'She's bringing bagels for lunch, remember? And she'll put some other things in the ward fridge for emergencies. I really think she'll be alright. It's only six days.'

'I can't imagine what she was thinking of,' argued my father, shaking with anger suddenly, 'crossing Merrion Avenue on her own like that. How could she have thought that was a good idea? Her eyesight's awful! She can barely see!' A baffled expression settled on Adrian's face now, as if Grandma Lily was Stanmore's answer to the Bermuda Triangle.

'Yes, well, she's made a mistake, hasn't she?' said Mum. 'And thank goodness it's only a broken leg. She's been lucky, Adrian, and she'll recover in no time. Look, it's not necessary for you to stay in London. We've been looking forward to this holiday for such a long time.'

'Yes, you're right, Lo-lo,' said my father, still twitching. 'She'll be alright. I'm sure she will. It's just that I feel so guilty.'

§

Grandpa Jožka and Grandma Lotka were waiting as usual at Arosa station, wearing fur hats, shades and huge smiles. My sister and I were excited to see them after our long journey, and we each took a grandparent by the hand for the stroll to the hotel. As we walked, I kept an eye open for Greta Garbo. You never knew. A deer-like glance, hypnotic eyes, a sidling gait; every old woman that passed became her for an instant.

Grandpa showed us to our rooms, announcing, 'Welcome to the best hotel in Arosa.' Then the four of us were alone again.

'Did you notice,' said Mum, 'how my parents didn't say a single word to each other?'

'Now you mention it,' said Adrian.

'They must be in the middle of an argument. My mother didn't even kiss me hello. Why does she have to be so distant?'

'Oh, that's just her. You know what she's like.'

'Yes, but to not even touch me?'

'Look, Lo-lo, I must just phone Edgware General. I can't relax until I've done it.'

Mum raised her eyes to heaven. I shrugged my shoulders in return, conveying that she and I were in sync; on the exact same page about the kind of husband Dad had turned into.

'Are you alright, Mum?' Dad squeaked down the receiver. 'The food OK?'

When the call ended, Dad's face changed completely, and his voice went normal.

'She's fine,' he sighed. 'Feeling much better.'

'I'll feel better when you cut the umbilical cord,' said Mum.

The days were filled with skiing. Ruth and I had private lessons with a woman named Regula, who made everything fun and sang Sade's 'Smooth Operator' while we skied down. She laughed a lot and had an American accent even though she was Swiss. She wore the same blue outfit as the other teachers and lifted her ski pole to greet them. Sometimes she waved at people who were sunbathing and eating sausages in the open-air restaurants on the slopes.

In the afternoons we skied with our parents and with Grandpa Jožka, while Grandma Lotka went for mountain walks on her own or stayed at the hotel.

'But are you sure?' I asked my grandmother, each morning. 'Won't you get lonely?'

'Actually, it's nice to have a break,' she replied, cautiously eyeing her husband.

'She'll enjoy herself,' said Grandpa, with a flick of his hand. 'The staff here, they treat her like Cleopatra.'

*

The evenings were all about the hotel bar, where there was live music; mostly a crumpled German named Manfred who drank a lot of beer. Grandpa had a special relationship with him and would request the same Richard Clayderman number every night, which had a lot of frilly runs up and down the piano. Before he went to bed, Grandpa always stuck a banknote in Manfred's top pocket, and patted him on the back. Then he turned to us and said, 'The man's a drunkard.'

It turned out that my grandparents had made new friends that year: old Germans called Walter and Gertrud. They joined us for drinks. Adrian's first question: which city did they come from?

'Stuttgart,' they said, in unison.

'Oh, I have a postcard of the synagogue. You know it was destroyed during *Kristallnacht*?'

The two old Germans nodded sympathetically.

'You collect old photographs?' asked Walter.

'I have a large collection of postcards of European synagogues destroyed by the Nazis,' said Adrian. 'I also collect Jewish street life. The only thing I don't collect is anti-Semitica.'

The two Germans nodded gravely and blinked.

On the way back to our room, Adrian piped up, 'I just hope we don't have to spend any more evenings with Dr Mengele.'

'Oh, for goodness' sake. Not every German's a Nazi, you know.'

'Well, actually they were,' corrected Adrian. 'And if they weren't actively Nazis, they were complicit. Everyone knew about the concentration camps. How could they not? The Jews were being rounded up in the streets. It's well known that Volkswagen used Jewish slave labour, which is exactly why I would never buy a German car.'

'Adrian, can we please not talk about the Holocaust?' barked Mum. 'We're supposed to be on holiday.'

I threw Mum an exasperated look, like *why even waste your time on this joker?*

'I'm just saying that people knew, Anna.'

My father twitched his shoulders and adjusted his glasses, lost in thought. And as the lift groaned up to our floor, I had a thought of my own: I pictured old Walter with a swastika on his arm, doing the Hitler salute.

At night, I tried to grab a few moments to myself in the bedroom. Now that I'd been delivered the goods by puberty, I wanted to enjoy them to the max. I had strange fantasies of naked flesh and chalets and crisp mountain air, and making girls touch me. I flashed at myself in mirrors when no one was looking. It was like being the sole test driver of a brand-new car. I had dreams of naked skiing and Nazi stormtroopers and Greta Garbo sitting all alone on a chairlift, and me asking for her autograph. The two of us at the top of the Weisshorn, and her saying 'Vell possibly, just this vonce,' and me searching my salopettes for a pen but not being able to find one. Her shrugging at my tough luck, skiing off stylishly, back to her life of solitude, lifting up a ski pole to bid farewell.

At breakfast, Grandpa Jožka was praising the hotel again.

'It's the best breakfast here, no? They always have the best buffet. Now, may I cut up some fruit for my grandchildren?'

My sister and I nodded enthusiastically.

'And what do you think of the swimming pool? Also, the best, no?'

'Ach,' cut in Grandma Lotka, 'do we have to keep saying it's the best the whole time? How can one relax with such ongoing commentary?'

Grandpa Jožka threw his wife the blackest glance I'd seen, but she refused to catch his eye. Instead, she gave my hand a friendly smack and smiled broadly, as if she'd completely forgotten her husband was sitting beside her. Meanwhile, Mum quietly sipped her tea, turning her eyes from her father to her mother, then back again.

'Look who's here,' said Grandpa, pointing to the corner where Walter and Gertrud were breakfasting at their usual table.

Today, though, they had another exceedingly old woman at their table with them. Walter came over to explain.

'Don't stand up,' he instructed, leaning over my grandfather's shoulders. 'We have my wife's aunt with us for a few days. Tante Luise. She will stay indoors, mostly. We'll leave her at the hotel. She doesn't walk terribly well.'

The old woman, who was wearing lacy white gloves, seemed to know she was being talked about, and wiggled two fingers in our direction, opening her eyes wide. Greta Garbo? Shape of the face was familiar – arched eyebrows. I couldn't be sure. If she wanted to be on her own?

'And now I shall let you enjoy the rest of your breakfast.' Walter nodded and returned to his table.

'He's a nice chap,' said Grandpa. 'Very decent. You know he apologized to me last night – for being a German.'

'Apologized?' Adrian seemed interested. 'Well, that's something, I suppose.'

'Yes. And I told him, "If you did nothing wrong, Walter, then there's no need to apologize." And he thanked me. He even kissed me! Can you imagine such a thing?' Grandpa blinked and shook his head from side to side.

If the old woman was Greta Garbo, I considered, she'd have room service. It made no sense to risk being recognized at the breakfast bar. She'd sit in her room watching black-and-white films of herself as a young beauty and flick off as soon as the knock came at the door.

§

It was Saturday night. We left Dad in the room phoning Grandma Lily and went down to the bar. Walter and Gertrud and the other old German woman were sitting together in the corner with my grandparents. The Germans were smoking brightly coloured cigarillos, and the really ancient woman lifted up her hand again and wiggled her fingers.

The hotel had organized a special band called Black & White, which consisted of a drummer who was black and a keyboard player who was white. They smiled and nodded at each other at the end of each number, which always finished with White doing a cha-cha-cha on the keyboard and Black doing a cymbal crash. They played 'I Just Called to Say I Love You' and 'The Birdie Song' – my sister and I did the actions, linked arms and twirled each other around in fast circles – then 'You are the Sunshine of My Life', which was when my grandfather held out his hand for his wife to dance with him. Grandma Lotka acceded to the request but looked distracted by private thoughts as Grandpa guided her across the floor.

My sister and I weren't about to do a smoochy dance together, so headed back to our table to join Mum. Which was when I noticed Walter approaching Grandpa and tapping him on the shoulder. He whispered something, then they both looked over at me and my grandfather beckoned me over.

'My favourite grandson,' he said. 'Walter's aunt, this Tante Luise, she's been watching you, and she wants very much to have a little dance.'

The ancient German woman was staring at me from across the room, smiling and nodding as if she already knew what Grandpa was saying.

'With me? I don't want to, Grandpa! Please don't make me.'

'But she is all alone,' said Grandpa, with a pleading look in his eye. 'A poor old widow. Come on. Be a man. Do it for Grandpa.' With that, he beckoned Tante Luise over as if I'd just agreed to everything.

The only place for me to put my hand was on the old woman's waist. I could feel folds of loose skin underneath her dress, and her body was icy cold. Her breathing was heavy and raspy. Then I noticed the smell. It was coming from her mouth. Not from cigarettes – much worse – like something rotting inside her body.

'I feel like this is the beginning,' sang Black & White, 'though I've loved you for a million years . . .'

As we turned around the dance floor, I thought, *This isn't Garbo. More like Dr Mengele's wife. Garbo's back in New York, leafing through photographs of yesteryear.* I imagined the old actress signing autographs for herself, just for the fun of it – to spite me. 'For Greta, thanks for the memories, Greta Garbo.' She'd tear them up, laughing, then throw them in the trash.

When the song ended, the old woman let go suddenly and clapped her hands towards Black & White. She offered Grandpa a big overhead wave and walked back to her friends, rejuvenated, not leaning on the chairs as much as before. Adrian had arrived on scene now, his Kodak hanging loose around his neck. I supposed he had to have seen me dancing with the old German woman, because he looked pale, like he'd seen a ghost. Now Grandpa was calling something out to the three Germans and nodding profusely, I guessed saying something complimentary about me. They faced him in a line, bowing their heads stiffly, like tired old politicians at the end of a long meeting.

I joined my sister at the table, then Grandpa made his way over.

'I'm so proud of you,' he said.

He reached to stroke my cheek, but I pulled away and refused to catch his eye.

'You made an old widow so happy,' he chirped. 'Now, my grandson, will you stay up tonight and play bingo?'

Tonight? A nice suggestion, but I didn't think so. I spotted my father teeing up his Kodak for a pensive portrait so held up my hand. No photos, please! I wasn't in the mood. In fact, I wasn't going to be schmoozed or bamboozled for a second longer.

'I'm going to my room,' I announced. 'I vont to be alone.'

RAY CHARLES

My music had roots which I'd dug up
from my own childhood, musical roots
buried in the darkest soil.

Ray Charles

I was fourteen and heard that Ray Charles would be performing at the Barbican. This set my autograph mind whirring. Ray was beyond tough; Ray was a nightmare. If you wrote, all you ever got was a secretarial signed photo, in perfect handwriting:

All the best, Ray Charles

in fast-flowing ink to the light spot of the image, so it stood out. The man was blind. When you wrote back, clarifying you were after a hand-signed autograph by the great man himself, it only ever prompted the arrival of another even closer-up shot of Ray singing at the piano, with the same old secretarial scrawl.

These fake Rays were all I ever saw until *The Inkwell* published a signature study showing several of his actual autographs discovered from the 1950s. Back then, he sometimes signed for fans in pointy block capitals; nothing like the flowing ink on those publicity photos. Very few authentic Rays had ever surfaced. He'd stopped signing, overnight, in 1960, and all anyone had seen since was the flowery secretarial affair.

Ray's had become an autograph I wanted badly, in the special kind of psychotic way that autograph collectors wanted the things they couldn't have. I wanted Ray's autograph because it was unobtainable, because he didn't want me to have it. But I also wanted it because I'd grown to love the man. I loved the gravel in his voice, his immutability, his remorselessness. I admired him for the centuries of suffering he injected into his musical phrasing, for his ability to turn 'Eleanor Rigby' into a pacy, confessional blues anthem.

I'd learnt piano since the age of eight and was on grade six now. My lessons were with a nervy Pinner woman who lived in a neat house with charts on the wall for her young son, with ticks and gold stars. She'd tell me to "sharpen" my fingertips and practise everything very slowly with a metronome. My sister played too, and sometimes we did a duet – Handel's 'Arrival of the Queen of Sheba'. The plonky left hand made us laugh our heads off. We'd play and laugh simultaneously and crash our way to the end.

Other times, I'd sit at the piano with a tape recorder, stopping and starting it till I'd taught myself how to play the introduction to 'Makin' Whoopee' the way Ray did it – fully flat-fingered. There was something uncompromising about his timing that I wanted to capture but could never quite get right. My version lagged in a lazy suburbs of North London way, while his spiked with danger. I tried shutting my eyes and being blind, but that didn't help. I tried focusing on slavery, but that didn't help either. I tried playing as if I didn't care about anyone but myself, as if I didn't even *want* to see, as if I'd happily have someone sign photographs on my behalf and send them to unsuspecting nine-year-old cancer sufferers in Pinner.

Now I was getting somewhere.

'Very good,' Adrian said, taking a break from reorganizing his Hungarian synagogues. 'You know, some day, when Ruth's an academic, or I don't know, a lawyer maybe, you'll be playing the piano in a little cocktail bar somewhere and you'll be really happy.'

'Thanks, Dad. I'm not sure I want to be a cocktail pianist.'

'Yes, well, something else then. What I'm saying is, whatever you decide to do is completely OK with me. You might be a film director or a cartoonist, and that would be no problem. Or if you decided you wanted to be a pornographer, that would also be fine.'

§

Ever since breaking her leg, Grandma Lily had become a serious problem. We'd entered a new phase, because Adrian said she couldn't live alone any more. She was no longer safe. Anna pointed out that Lily was better able to cope than Adrian realized, that she exaggerated her poor eyesight so he'd worry about her more. That made me think of the games of rummy my sister and I played with our grandma, how she pretended not to notice when I cheated, but always somehow knew.

'What's going to happen, exactly?' Anna asked, exasperated. 'So, she slips over and dies. She's got to die of something eventually, hasn't she? She's eighty. She's had a good innings.'

But Adrian was concerned, and gave Anna the job of finding someone to live with his mother. A stream of au pair girls followed. They arrived youthful and smiling, nodding their heads amiably at the long list of duties and caveats agreed between Adrian and Lily. They left weeks later, gibbering wrecks with bloodshot eyes. There turned out to be a few additional rules added by Lily herself: a draconian evening curfew of 6.45 p.m., no friends over at any time, and strictly no ingoing or outgoing phone calls just in case Adrian might be trying to get through.

'What I'd love best is to live with you all,' poor blind

Grandma Lily explained one day, twisting the age-old gambit into a gentle question with her hand. 'These au pair girls are no company. We sit in silence. I wait all day for the phone to ring, and it never does. Nobody comes and nobody phones.'

'Mum,' said Anna, 'Adrian phones you every single day.'

'That's different,' said Lily. 'He's always in such a rush.'

'Look, Mum. We need to make it work with one of these girls, don't we? Otherwise, Adrian is going to have to think about moving you somewhere he *knows* you'll be safe.'

'Not a home! I won't go to a home! A home is a place you go to die!'

Anna narrowed her eyes at Adrian, then opened her hands as if to say, *Can't you see what she's doing?*

Mum got so tired of Adrian's pleasureless relationship with his mother that she created a new rule of her own. If he was going to ring her every day, he'd have to do it from his car phone. She'd had enough. She didn't want to hear her husband's strained voice. So now, when Adrian got home from work, he sat in the front driveway with the engine running, holding his face and deep breathing till he managed to steer Grandma Lily to the end of another circular conversation.

It was around this time my father began to work longer hours in the West End. He saw clients early in the morning as well as in the evening. Sometimes he went Israeli dancing twice a week, and he began working on Saturdays.

'It's so much easier to get things done when no one's in the office,' he clarified, racing down the staircase for dear life one Saturday morning at 7 a.m.

'But if you work most nights *and* you work on Saturdays *and* you make us see your mother on Sundays, when exactly are we supposed to spend time just the two of us?' Anna would ask. 'This isn't a normal life, Adrian. I didn't sign up for this.'

'Oh, it's not that bad,' he retorted, furiously brushing his curls. 'You have no idea how much pressure I'm under. There's just so much paperwork to get through. And my secretaries are all useless.'

'If they're useless, then why don't you sack them and get better ones?'

'Oh, I couldn't! I'd feel too guilty.'

'You're absent, Adrian – can't you see? And I spend all my time procuring au pair girls for your mother. This isn't a marriage. It's a bad dream.'

'I'm sorry, Lo-lo. As soon as I get on top of the backlog at the office, I promise we'll spend more time together.'

Adrian stroked Mum's cheek and flew out the front door, while I looked down from the upstairs banister, wondering if it was really paperwork or useless secretaries or even Grandma Lily that was the problem.

§

I got my parents to book tickets for the Ray Charles concert at the Barbican and counted down the days. I notified my pen pal Yogesh Gupta. He couldn't attend himself, due to ophthalmological obligations at the Newcastle Infirmary, so sent photocopies of duplicates from his collection that he'd consider trading for an authentic Ray. But I had no intention of swapping a Ray for a Sinatra or even a Schulz sketch. I'd keep it in my collection and send copies of myself holding it to Yogesh and the others. Darren Pendle was particularly circumspect. He said there was no way Ray would sign, because he'd made the top-ten-worst-signers list for the past ten years.

On the day of the concert, I decided on a two-pronged attack: I would try to get him to sign before the concert, then if that failed, I'd try again at the end. I brought my autograph book and pen and arrived two hours early to case the joint. I tried the main stage door first. A group of fans were there waiting. Miserable-looking musicians arrived carrying instruments in 'RC BAND' cases. World-weary and unsmiling, they dragged their boxes and bags through the door like holidaymakers checking in to a one-star motel. Now a group of scary women with big hair huffed their way through, unencumbered by instruments. These had to be Ray's backing singers, the Raelettes, the ones who were always telling him to hit the road. I remembered the singer had once boasted, 'To be a Raelette, you've got to let Ray.'

I figured the great man would resent arriving through this entrance with all the riff raff. He'd want his own private door. So, I worked my way around to the back of the Barbican, in search of a hidden entrance. Sure enough, a black car soon pulled up to what looked like a secret stage door within the car park. And, wait a minute, the back door of the car was opening, and a man in dark glasses was emerging. I ran towards him, clutching my autograph book.

'Mr Charles,' I called out, 'could you please sign this?'

It was Ray Charles, alright, but he was in no mood to break bread.

'I don't sign nothin' for no one!' he yapped.

I felt small. I felt told. I felt undeterred.

'Please?' I implored.

I was a child, for God's sake. OK, fourteen. But still a

child. And children were sweet. Besides, I was the only fan there. One single fan. After one single autograph. Ray Charles was undeterred himself. He walked towards the entrance with a stony expression on his face, a helper on his arm. He'd dealt with worse shit than this. He'd been arrested for possession of heroin. He'd had ten children with ten different pissed-off women.

As he disappeared through the door, he couldn't resist yelling out to me, 'I can't write, anyhow.' And I could have sworn I heard a chuckle as he disappeared from view.

Chuckle, because he knew he was lying. I'd seen his signature.

The concert was great and everything. At the start, Ray came hobbling onto the stage, aided by his helper. The audience clapped but seemed worried about the physical state of their idol. Was this a sympathy tour? But Ray was monkeying around, once he'd positioned himself in front of the piano stool, he threw himself violently backwards onto it and smashed his hands down on the keyboard and started ripping up a tune. The crowd loved that, and he gained my grudging respect too.

As Ray grinned himself into a twelve-bar blues, I started to formulate my strategy for the end of the show. I'd go back and try again. But how to get this autograph without calling a blind man a liar? I was in a tight spot.

Next, Ray got into his stride with renditions of 'What'd I Say' and 'You Don't Know Me'. Was it my imagination, or did this band have as much beef with the singer as I did? They looked rigid and joyless, like prison inmates taking part in a performance for the screws. A charming duet with an exhausted-looking Raelette followed – 'Baby It's Cold Out-side' – essentially a song about date rape.

I had a thought. I would call Ray's bluff. So, he says he can't write. But, surely, he'd be capable of leaving his *mark*?

When the concert ended, Ray was given the expected ovation, and while all the bowing and ceremony took place, I turned to my parents and sister.

'I'm heading to the stage door,' I barked. 'Meet me there.' And I was off.

Again, I was the sole fan standing at the secret entrance. Before long, there was a commotion, and I positioned myself such that Ray would be forced into a full body slam with me upon exit. His huge bodyguard was having none of it. He put his flat hand against me and pushed me back.

'Mr Charles,' I shouted, and I could see from a movement in the singer's head that he recognized my voice from earlier.

'I told you. I can't write!'

'Well, if you can't write, could you just sign with a cross?'

There. Not my proudest moment, but what other chance would I get?

'I told you no,' yelled Ray. 'I don't sign!'

'Yes, but could you just . . .'

'What's your name?'

This was Ray's bodyguard talking now. He was enormous, and in my face, and as far as I could tell about to break my fourteen-year-old-child legs. There was only so much shit Ray would take before he took you down.

'Adam,' I murmured.

The bodyguard seized the pen out of my hand, then took my autograph book from me. Was it being confiscated? I was getting ready to kick up a fuss. *Hey, that's got John Malkovich in there,* I'd protest. *And six Michael Winners!* The body-guard opened the book and flicked to a blank page, then started writing something. Which seemed odd. Was he writing out a formal warning? A restraining order?

'There you go,' the bodyguard said. He returned the book to me, and bundled Ray into the back of the vehicle.

As the car screeched off, and Ray took a well-earned break from all the horrible exposure to the general public, I stood in the road and opened my autograph book.

There it was again – the fast-flowing ink.

'To Adam, best wishes, Ray Charles.'

'Very unfair because you know he *can* write,' said Dad in the Volvo. 'Why wouldn't he just give you his autograph? Very frustrating.'

My sister and I were in the back watching the long, grey, flat buildings of the Barbican drift by. The windscreen wipers went on.

'Maybe it's an issue of trust,' suggested Mum. 'He can't see what he's signing.'

'Or maybe he just doesn't like signing autographs,' suggested Ruth.

'I'm not sure it's any of that,' I said. 'I think he doesn't like the idea of visual symbols. He's a musician. He puts everything he has into sound.'

I tried to imagine Ray collecting postcards of slaves working on plantations just to have a "record" and to show his friends, and thought, why collect something that's already in you?

Dad was fiddling around to find a CD to put on, and I noticed that new twitch again, the one he'd developed around the shoulders. I saw Mum notice it too; a concerned look appeared on her lips. It made me wonder how well she'd cope when my sister went to university the next year, and how things would be two years after that when I was gone myself and she was left all alone with The Adrian and Lily Show.

'Listen to this,' said Dad.

It was the Everly Brothers' 'Wake Up, Little Susie', and Dad started singing along, providing the guitar riff as well as the main tune.

As the Volvo cruised down the Hendon Way, then through Stanmore, I meditated on Ray Charles's childhood of poverty: a blind black child with an absent father in the America of the 1930s. When he was fifteen, his mother died and he began a musical career, grief-stricken. He later described how music had been a part of his body, like his ribs or liver. 'From the moment I learnt that there were piano keys to be mashed, I started mashing 'em, trying to make sounds out of feelings.' I realized that Ray and I were still connected, if not through his autograph then through his music. And his playing told stories about how I felt about *my* life, too; about my own absent father and exhausted mother; about the generations of suffering that had led my father to collect postcards of destroyed synagogues and my mother to create sculptures that drew your attention elsewhere, outside the camera frame of everyday life. His music made all those connections. And Ray and I had argued, to boot. What could be better?

The car lurched through Hatch End, then left onto our road, where our detached red-brick house stood. Dad backed the Volvo in beside Mum's Honda, then leant his hand on the car phone, saying, 'I'll be in soon. I must just ring my mother.'

'Your mother?' Mum had a paralysed look on her face. She seemed too exhausted to argue.

'Sorry, Lo-lo. She'll be waiting to hear from me. I can't *not* phone her. She'll worry. Look, I didn't have time before the concert because I was picking you up. And it was mayhem at the office – I couldn't find a moment. Look, I won't be long, I promise.'

Mum's keys rattled as she opened the front door. The three of us went inside and stepped across the brown carpet. Our family's visual symbols were arranged around the hall, the items that painted a picture of our happy Pinner life together: Mum's sculptures and a few bits of Dad's favourite framed artwork: stylized rabbis and synagogues and a carica-ture of me and my sister hanging out of a San Francisco tram. Ruth went upstairs to her room, which had cloud wallpaper and was full of books, while I put my autograph album down on the hall table and went up to my room at the front of the house. Mine was the one with the view down onto the drive, the green carpet and the Teddy Bears' picnic wallpaper.

I looked out of the bay window, down onto the front drive, and saw Dad in his car, hunched over the car phone, a hand half across the receiver.

MILES DAVIS

I have to change.
It's like a curse.

Miles Davis

In Pinner United Synagogue with my father on Yom Kippur. Our once-a-year pilgrimage, side by side with the other fathers and sons. It was an Orthodox shul, so the service was in Hebrew and no one had a clue what was going on – apart from the rabbi and my atheist father, both shokeling enthusiastically towards the ark. Adrian was wearing trainers, because this was the one day of the year you were supposed to forgo "luxuries".

'We're not religious,' I snarled, when leaving the house. 'You don't even believe in God. These trainers look ridiculous with my suit. I'm wearing leather shoes.'

Complaining about synagogue was a tradition stretching back as far as I could remember. That year, Dad delivered his usual lecture on how vital it was we attend a shul like ours, with a service that hadn't changed for two thousand years, because of "continuity". A synagogue like the Brichtos' was closer to a church, he insisted, waving a finger, because it had an organ and a choir, and the service took an hour and a half instead of the correct three.

'And the worst thing is the rabbi standing with his back to the ark. Everyone knows you don't do *that*.'

The other fathers, who were accountants, solicitors and financial advisors, sat very still beside their sons, who had names like Wayne and Toby and Russell, and sported matching hairdos to their fathers. I was hoping my short-back-and-sides was making a good enough case against the Leo Sayer Afro beside me.

'I must tell you a joke,' said Dad to the nearest father–son team, 'about the Jewish woman who goes to the travel agent. Have you heard it? "Last year I went on a world cruise," she says. "This year I'd like to go somewhere different!"'

My father's face crumpled at his own joke, then the other dad, who had thin lips and pale skin and was surely a relative of Dracula, offered a neat smile. The vampire's son stared morosely into the mid-distance, grappling with a future in accountancy.

'I've heard that joke at least a hundred times,' I said, aping my mother, averting my gaze from the whole embarrassing spectacle.

Now that Ruth was studying Law at Durham, Mum was forced to sit alone somewhere towards the back of the women's section. She'd raised the usual objections on the walk down: how the other women always prattled through the service; how whenever the rabbi shushed them, they started up again.

'So, you'd rather sit in silent contemplation?' snapped Dad, as we sloped past Pinner tandoori. 'You'd rather sit in a church?'

'Northwood Liberal Synagogue is not a church, Adrian.'

Things were not marvellous between my parents now that Ruth had gone. My father basically lived in the Volvo. You caught sight of him in the early morning, or at night, twitching in front of the news, inhaling a snatched meal while Mum slept upstairs. Other than that, he was lithe, on the move; visiting clients or Judaica postcard dealers, or Israeli folk dancing. We barely heard a thing from my sister in Durham, where she was up to her eyeballs in Law, and the brief conversations between my parents were essentially speculations on how she might be getting on there. The consensus was that silence equalled love interest – a cause of great consternation to my father.

'If she's found a boyfriend, doesn't he have a name?' he demanded of Mum.

'I'm sure he has a name.'

'It's probably Chris.'

'Oh, for goodness' sake, Adrian. This isn't the 1890s. We're not living in a shtetl. Anyway, you're just jealous.'

'Jealous? What are you talking about?' Dad trembled and rearranged himself, and his eyes darted around like Rasputin.

If I wasn't tuning in to my parents' relationship, I was combing through my autograph collection, writing letters to celebrities, practising the piano or listening to jazz. I was on grade seven now, but jazz was where my heart lay. I bought a trove of new CDs and relegated my old pop cassettes to the top cupboard of my bedroom. My favourite album was now Miles Davis's *Kind of Blue*. When I first heard it, I had no idea that music like that existed; the opening bars of 'So What', where the double bass poses musical questions, and the rest of the band respond with a "so what" motif.

I was fascinated by improvisation, the overlaying of spontaneous notes on known tunes. Whenever I tried it myself, it sounded cardboard and clichéd, and caused my father to make his cocktail pianist comments. So, I bought a book of Bill Evans piano transcriptions – he was the pianist on *Kind of Blue* – and practised them the same way I might a Mozart or Beethoven sonata.

As far as jazz autographs were concerned, I had a few: Oscar Peterson, Ella Fitzgerald and Dave Brubeck. All three sent signed photos. Vintage jazz autographs were a rarity, because jazz greats tended to die young of drug abuse, and were poor, which meant they hadn't had publicity photos or fan clubs. A lot weren't even famous during their lifetimes, so the autographs that surfaced were impromptu ones given in person at clubs.

I'd written to Miles Davis a bunch of times without reply. Word was, he didn't sign by post. If you met him in person he might comply, depending on his mood. In the 1950s, he wrote his full name – I'd seen a few examples. But these days, all he ever put was 'Miles' with a musical note, which felt like his way of saying that he was no longer the same person he'd once been, back in the day. Lately I'd been reading his autobiography, which was unlike any book I'd read before. There was more swearing on page one than the total number of printed expletives I'd encountered to date. I felt it could have benefited from its own glossary of terms:

Motherfucker = Fantastic guy
Shit = Great
Bullshit = Amazing
Terrible = Out of this world
Motherfucker (variant) = Motherfucker

Miles even put in a photograph of someone he hated, just so he could label it, 'Now, he was one motherfucker I never liked.' I was intoxicated by Miles's nerve. He knew what he thought and didn't care if he offended. The son of a middle-class dentist, Miles had a classical training on the trumpet, but when he heard Charlie Parker, that was it; he moved away from everything. The past didn't exist for him. He wasn't interested in yesterday. Not just because of his run-ins with racist police and drug addiction, but on principle. He wasn't the nostalgic type, which was why his musical style kept changing, and why, these days, he was doing cover versions of Cyndi Lauper and Michael Jackson tracks. But, man, he was playing that bullshit like a terrible motherfucker. Everyone loved it. I loved it.

What intrigued me most about his playing was his unpredictability. You never knew where a musical phrase might lead. I tried guessing, but he surprised me every time. I figured, here was a man who refuses to be known in that way. And that refusal interested me, because it asked questions of its own, like: *Why would you even _want_ to predict someone's moves?* And: *Who would you be without your predictions?* I didn't have answers to these questions, but I was hooked on the mystery. Miles was one big refusal, a ball of restlessness who'd changed the course of jazz. Restless and resistant, yet there was that whole world of feeling in his playing. He spoke not only of the black-American experience, but of so much beyond. He was the everyman. You could hear it all if you listened correctly, if you stopped trying to predict.

§

Things got worse between my parents when a group of young Russian Israeli dance fanatics passed through London, and Adrian suggested driving them around to see the sights and generally have a good time. It turned into a night-time tour of Westminster, and he developed dozens of photographs of Russian teens posing in the back of his Volvo, sipping canned drinks.

'Who's that?' Mum asked, squinting.

'That's Galina. Didn't you meet her in Hatfield?'

'Can't say I did. And who are these?'

'Oh, that's Irina and Annika. You don't know them? They did the sketch with the balalaika – remember?'

'So, what's a forty-four-year-old insurance broker doing driving Russian teenagers around the West End? Are you having some kind of crisis, Adrian?'

'Not at all, Lo-lo. Don't be silly. Look, I'd love to discuss this with you, but I must just phone my mum.'

Then there was my father announcing to my mother that she wasn't invited to the staff Christmas party, because spouses "in general" weren't being included. He said she shouldn't feel bad, because she wouldn't enjoy it. Oh, and now he planned to go on *two* different residential Israeli dance camps in the summer, the second to be held in Budapest, which had the added attraction that he could drive around looking for the sites of synagogues whose postcards he owned. He could see if any of the synagogues were still standing, take photos of them, then compare them to his postcards.

'Well, have a marvellous time,' said Mum. 'I'm not coming. I can't take any more of your synagogues.'

'But it would be so exciting to find them,' Adrian insisted. 'I was thinking, maybe I could create a book showing my old postcards alongside modern-day photographs of the buildings that are still standing. Could be an important record.'

'Oh, for goodness' sake. It's always got to be *you* in the middle of things, hasn't it? You know what? I'm not going to Budapest, Adrian, and I'm not going to Hatfield. There's only so much of this madness I can take.'

The next day, a Saturday, when Dad was at the office and Mum was playing tennis, my curiosity got the better of me. I had a root around the study to see what incriminating evidence I could find on my father. It was a room only he ever went into, not least because it was full of smelly collector's albums and books about synagogues, housed in falling-down bookcases, alongside ancient auction catalogues of Palestine postal history. In the corner was an old briefcase with a three-digit combination lock.

When 111, 123 and 999 all failed, I decided to try every single combination until I got the right one. How long could it take? It took half an hour. At one point, I thought I heard the front door open and froze in terror, but it was only the postman. Then, finally, it clicked open. Out popped an ancient-looking calling card for a strip club and an autograph letter, hand-addressed to my father at his office, with a recent postal stamp. I opened this up, and quickly read it. The handwriting was curvy and childish. It was from a woman in the Netherlands by the name of Flore. Something about Israeli dancing, then a line that went: 'I can't wait to be with you, Adrian, and to love you again.' I felt a deep, horrible clunk in my stomach, as though a tectonic plate deep within me was twisting into a new and painful position. *Love you again*? I hurriedly put everything back in the briefcase; tried to catch my breath.

What to do? I pictured my mother's face, how a trauma like this might destroy her. When she saw *Fatal Attraction*, she didn't like the ending because the Michael Douglas character wasn't punished enough. 'If someone were to cheat on *me*,' she warned, eyeing Dad, 'that would be it.' So, would she now divorce my father? Could she cope alone? What would happen to me? I envisioned myself floating, untethered, between sky and earth. Who would a person be if their two halves no longer fitted together?

When my father came home that night, Mum was in the kitchen, and Dad jogged upstairs to get changed.

'I found your love letter,' I said. I was waiting for him in his bedroom, trembling. My heart was pumping, and the sounds of my mother clattering around downstairs were distorted. 'In your briefcase, in the study.'

'What do you mean?' asked Dad, blinking and smiling. He closed the bedroom door behind him.

'A letter from a Dutch woman, saying she wants to love you again.' The plates shifted in my stomach while I searched my father's face for the truth.

He was silent for a moment, then his smile fully died. He started doing the shoulder twitch and covered his mouth with his hand.

'Nothing happened,' he hissed through his fingers. He took a breath, then leant towards me. 'The girl had a crush, that's all – a silly girl from Amsterdam.' He was speaking quite calmly and deliberately now, as if reciting a prayer. 'And there was only one kiss. I promise you. I wouldn't even call it a kiss. I just brushed her lips when I said goodbye – that was it. It was all just silly.'

'But it didn't sound like that, Dad. It sounded like more.'

'I should never have kept the letter. Nothing happened, Doobs. And, listen. It's very important you don't tell your mother. If you tell her, she'll only try and stop me going to the dance camp. So, please don't. OK?'

I kept my distance from my father for a while. I listened to the smouldering sounds of Miles instead. I felt terrible pangs of guilt every time my mother made a trip to the supermarket or prepared a meal that went cold because Dad was working late. I hadn't believed my father's version – not really – and was pretty sure my mother wouldn't. *If someone were to cheat on me, that would be it.* Sometimes I'd be in my room, listening to Miles, and an argument would start downstairs. I couldn't hear the words, but the cadences of the voices were familiar enough, told me which standard they were performing: the one about Ruth's boyfriend, the one about Grandma Lily or the one about how Dad was never there, had turned into a stranger. I continued to play Bill Evans transcriptions on the piano, and made friends listen to my diatribes about improvisation: how Miles Davis didn't want to be *known* by the listener, just wanted to be listened to; how Miles didn't care for the past, how the past was all tyranny. I practised my piano pieces with the metronome, and my fingers flew up and down the keyboard, somehow knowing where to go and what to do without me even consciously controlling them. I ran and reran my father's voice saying, 'Don't tell your mother.' Don't tell her what? If there's nothing to tell, what's the secret?

§

Miles at the Hammersmith Odeon, leaning on his bass player Foley's shoulders. Foley was wearing a bandanna, had horizontal rips all the way down his jeans, and I was there with a girl named Rachel. We hadn't kissed yet, and we weren't going out officially, but she was really pretty, although not strictly speaking a jazz fan. I suspected she'd come to the concert because she liked me. Miles's trumpet was down and into Foley's chest, and the sound was like a wheeze, then a whine. He was telling Foley something, and you could hear a remnant of his best stuff – who he had once been in the 1950s. The stage was alive with colour, not least Miles's shiny suit jacket and the blue spotlights. The bass guitar was ringing in my ears. I had the thought, 'From son of a dentist to this.' Then, 'From son of an insurance broker to . . .?' For a moment, I was ecstatic. I was in the moment. But then came another thought: the house in Pinner where I'd soon return. Mum standing alone in the kitchen. Dad slamming the front door, and my listening in to the cadences of their conversation.

What I hadn't expected was that Miles would spend the entire concert with his back to the audience. A man a few rows behind yelled, 'Turn around, Miles' a few times, but I didn't think he heard. Not that it would have made any difference. Personally, I had no problem with his turned back, because I knew it was Miles's way of staying true to himself: focusing on his music, on the band, refusing to be swayed by outside expectation. He played Michael Jackson's 'Human Nature' and Cyndi Lauper's 'Time after Time', and whenever his band members played a solo, he put his arm over their shoulder as if they were under his personal care and free to express themselves in any way they wished. After an hour of music, I noticed Miles casually strolling off the stage just when the drummer started playing a long, intricate solo.

'He's leaving,' I bleated at Rachel. 'He's not coming back. Let's go.'

We made our way to the stage door and, sure enough, Miles Davis was already emerging. The concert was ongoing, yet he was already heading back to his hotel. So incredibly Miles. I'd come armed with a stack of cards and a felt-tip pen. There would have been no use bringing my *Kind of Blue* album; he refused to sign old images of himself. If I was lucky, I'd get a simple "Miles" signature, with a musical note. Chances were, I wouldn't even get that.

He was shielded as he got into his limo, then one of his helpers offered to hand in items for him to sign while he was seated there. I watched his hand penning his name on two of my cards, then they were handed back to me. "Miles Davis", he'd written.

'He's signed his full name!' I yelled at Rachel, elated.

Then Miles did another thing he never did, something I could never have anticipated. He held his hand up to the limousine window and smiled.

§

My father was following the service with his usual solicitousness, licking a finger as he turned the pages of our prayer book, muttering in Hebrew. I knew he knew the service this well because at the age of nineteen, when his father died, he became religious for a while, to honour his father's passing. Going to synagogue twice a day became important to him, and he grew a long beard during the year of mourning. According to Mum, he'd felt guilty at that time, because he hadn't treated his father with the proper respect during his later years – it had been frustrating to have a father who was suffering with Parkinson's, and shaking and falling over all the time. But Adrian hadn't realized quite how ill his father was, and then it was suddenly over – his father died. I sometimes wondered if that was why he collected synagogues: as a way of trying to apologize.

But I was feeling low on sympathy.

We were coming towards the bit in the service when you were supposed to repent for your sins. You grabbed a handful of prayer shawl and banged yourself on your chest.

I got the dig in the ribs.

'Come on, Doobs. Stand.'

'Everyone's still sitting,' I replied. I wanted to add "motherfucker", but I restrained myself. It was true, though, that only a handful of people had got to their feet so far. Why did we have to be the first? And, anyway, what did *I* have to repent for? I thought of the letter from the Dutch woman. Didn't my father have a few sins of his own to attend to?

'They're wrong,' barked my father, angrily pulling at my sleeve. 'You're supposed to stand for this bit. What's got into you?'

'I can't be bothered!' I retorted. I stayed seated, while all the men stood up around me.

My father's face bore down on me. My refusal wasn't part of our Yom Kippur script. I could see him searching himself for a way to make me cooperate.

'You stand up, Adam. Out of respect for me! Stand up!'

NELSON MANDELA

We have waited too long
for our freedom.

Nelson Mandela

We were in a relationship, Rachel and I, which meant a lot of arguing, kissing and letter-writing. Like members of the French Resistance, we exchanged tear-stained notes each morning at 8.15 a.m. at Preston Road station. We journeyed south on the crowded Tube carriage in silence, me scouring my girlfriend's face for coded messages about the state of our romance. We parted company at Finchley Road Tube, then I read her latest letter on the walk up to school, devouring it greedily with my eyes. Rachel's epistolary style was atypical, ranging anywhere from *Times* cryptic crossword to Shakespearean soliloquy. I'd get a twist in my stomach if the sign-off was "luv" rather than "love" or if I found a reference to things getting too "intense". But four kisses or more at the end and I smiled at my spoils, strode up Arkwright Road with an air of conquest, a burning sensation descending into my loins.

It wasn't just Rachel I'd fallen for. I'd fallen for her parents.

Her father, Alvin, was a gentle soul who never tired of asking questions. He asked about school, about grandparents, about autographs, and listened to it all intently, slowly rocking his head.

'I'm not a collector, per se,' I explained, folding one leg over the other, sipping my tea. 'My dad's the real collector – he won't sell a single synagogue. I'm more of a dealer.'

'Oh, really,' said Rachel's dad. 'I see. Is that right?'

Alvin never retained the information and asked the same questions the next time around. Still, I was struck by the reliable quality of his listening. He only ever interrupted you to answer the phone or open a bottle of wine, then he sat right back down and said, 'Now, what were you telling me?'

If I made for the Tube after a Saturday evening spent in his daughter's bedroom, Alvin was having none of it.

'Don't be daft, I'll drop you home,' he said. 'It's nothing – five minutes down the road.'

This time frame became known as an "Alvin five minutes" because the journey, in fact, took twenty-five. Just as an "Alvin half an hour" was closer to three, and an "Alvin week" a month. The whole household seemed to operate according to these relaxed approximations of time and space. No one rushed around frantically brushing their hair, or rummaged around in drawers for magnifying glasses; they fell gently through life with the cheerful nonchalance of Alice down the rabbit hole; down, down, down, with no shortage of opportunity to glance around and get their bearings. Above all, there was no certainty at Rachel's house. No one ever wagged their finger at you about a fact.

There were, though, a lot of animals. Two cats and two dogs who wandered around the place panting, licking and scratching. Someone was forever letting a cat out the back or taking a dog up the road, and there was a genuine sense of these pets having citizens' rights. People advocated for them. 'I think Polly needs a wee,' someone would say, and someone else would say, 'Right. I'll take her.' When they reminisced about pets from the past, Rachel's mum, Maureen, would say, 'Oh, Penny was lovely – such a good-natured thing.'

Maureen was a tiny, powerful being, generally to be found instructing her husband, Alvin, to open said bottle of wine, or drive said boyfriend home. She was sharp-tongued and no nonsense, the kind of woman who'd think nothing of amputating a leg or delivering a stranger's baby. The toughness stemmed, ostensibly, from her being northern. Rachel's mum told anyone who'd listen about her idyllic childhood in Macclesfield, about the pubs her father frequented, the brands of cigarette he smoked, about the fourteen aunties she'd had. She sat me down and made me leaf through photo album after photo album, while Rachel fidgeted impatiently in the doorway.

'That one's Aunty Annie,' said Maureen, as if the woman with the round glasses and easy smile was my aunty too.

When she was done showing me her family photos, Maureen showed me Alvin's. He had little interest himself and struggled to remember the names of even his closest family members, but Maureen knew every single one. She prompted her husband to tell old stories, and when they fell apart halfway through she took over.

'My mum lost three babies,' explained Rachel, when Maureen left the room. 'When I was born, I was this huge miracle.'

She also explained how her mother had converted to Judaism, because it was the only way to get Alvin's parents to accept her, and because it made things less complicated for their one child, Rachel, whose enormous misty Shirley Temple portrait sat in a gilt frame on the living-room wall, presiding over proceedings like a child goddess.

'It's unbearable,' said Rachel, meaning the portrait. 'So idealized. Whenever I look at that photo, I think what a big disappointment the real me must be.'

'But you're gorgeous.'

'I'm not.'

'You are.'

At Rachel's house, the door knocker never stopped going. The people who turned up unannounced were drunk within minutes, leafing through photographs of Aunty Annie and the rest of the Macclesfield clan. The house was full of laughter. Alvin himself laughed so much that his face went red and he started coughing, especially if he was the butt of the joke. And Maureen had a high-pitched witter that she reserved for my driest gags about my father's collection of beer mats from pre-1948 hotels in Palestine, or Grandma Lily's latest spat with the au pair.

'Oh, you're wicked,' she said, touching my arm, shaking with laughter.

When we were done with the photo albums and stories, Rachel and I ensconced ourselves in her bedroom, kissing and cuddling and holding hands to Sting or Sinéad O'Connor's 'Nothing Compares to You'. From time to time, Alvin walked in without warning, offering tea, but really just spot-checking his daughter's chastity. Rachel and I quickly separated and feigned thoughtful, conversational poses.

'Dad! Maybe knock next time?' Rachel exclaimed. 'You're so intrusive!'

'Sorry, darling.' Alvin backed out of the room, obediently.

Eventually, Maureen called upstairs that dinner was ready, and we had chicken pie or a roast with all the trimmings.

'Come on, have some wine,' Maureen said, looming forth with a bottle.

'I'm fine,' I'd say, placing my hand over the glass, but the bottle still came.

'Come on. Just a splash. You might be dead tomorrow.'

*

I got home to find my parents watching *Sophie's Choice*, Mum threatening to go to bed and Dad simultaneously reorganizing his Polish synagogues, his glasses balanced on the end of his nose as if he was now a qualified professor of Genocidology.

'Meryl Streep's astonishingly versatile,' said Dad, partially looking up. 'Her accent's unbelievable. Nice evening, Doobs? What did you do?'

'Oh, nothing,' I said. 'I think I'll go upstairs.'

Ever since my discovery of the letter from the Dutch woman, I'd been doing my best to avoid Adrian. He, meanwhile, had been doing his best to corner me and reassure me how that letter meant precisely nothing. He said he felt dreadful about the whole thing, then triple-explained that the woman in question had had an inexplicable, naive crush; that nothing had happened; that he'd written to the girl to express outrage at her silly letter; that she wasn't even attractive; that in his experience the people who had affairs hid them so incredibly well that no one ever found out. I nodded and accepted these assurances, hoping to God – for my poor mother's sake – that at least one of these explanations was true. 'I'm not the kind of man who has an affair,' he concluded.

§

I practised the piano every day, because I had a school concert coming up: the first movement of Rachmaninoff's Second Piano Concerto with the school orchestra. I did scales and arpeggios and Hanon finger exercises with the metronome. While I rampaged through the thunderous introduction, I was filled with an uncanny conviction that with each crunch of harmony a small corner of the world was being put right. Sometimes, if my grandparents were over, Grandpa Jožka would appear at the door, hands held tight behind his back, and he would smile dreamily at the yearning melody. 'Beautiful,' he said, when I'd finished. 'Life is beautiful.'

When the concert came, I took my seat at the grand piano and felt like someone famous. My parents and sister and all three grandparents were there. I glanced into the audience, took a deep breath and dug into the opening bars.

Around this time, my mother decided to sculpt a portrait of me. I sat for her in the little studio at the back of the kitchen. My mother closed one eye and passed the other back and forth between her sixteen-year-old son and her wooden clay shaper. I stayed very still, breathing through my nose and enjoying my mother's gaze, filled with a sense of posterity.

'Gosh, your face has changed a lot recently,' she remarked, blinking her eyes. 'You have this new look of purpose.'

'You think?'

While my mother was sculpting, the usual sadness in her face went into remission. Instead, there was a flash of possibility, and I knew she wasn't thinking about synagogues or Dad's late-night meetings or her attempts to be understood by a man who couldn't understand things.

The sadness reliably returned later in the day, when she expressed doubts about how the portrait was going.

'I've got your chin wrong,' she lamented. 'Not sure. I think it needs to be bolder.'

'What are you talking about?' I exclaimed. 'It's going brilliantly. You've really captured something.'

'You think?'

Sometimes, while she worked, my mother talked about Dad, how his problems were down to his relationship with his controlling mother; how he'd never got over losing his father at such a young age.

'He had no model of how a father should be – that's the problem. And his parents had such an awful relationship. They even had physical fights. He witnessed some terrible things. The police would be called.'

I asked questions, just like Alvin, and nodded sympathetically, and wished my mother could experience something of the freedom of Rachel's family, where no one ever wasted time worrying about talent or limitations or tragedies from the past, and where there was nothing that couldn't be fixed with a glass of wine.

My mother and I dined together most evenings, discussing the links between music and sculpture. We talked about my potential as a musician, about the artistic process. I encouraged her to nurture her talents and make a proper go of things. I said, when I went to university, it would be no good her sitting around waiting for Dad. She simply had to find a new direction.

'I don't know,' my mother said. 'I should have more confidence.'

The front door would fly open at nine or ten, and Dad would burst in on us.

'I must show you the most amazing synagogue. In all my years of collecting, I've never seen this card.'

My mother and I would lock eyes, then slowly shake our heads.

§

Nelson Mandela had been on my mind for a while, especially since the seventieth-birthday tribute at Wembley two years earlier, when Tracy Chapman had wandered onstage like a busker and electrified everyone. I'd been writing to Mandela in prison ever since, enclosing photographs of him as a young man and asking him to sign, or asking vanilla questions about captivity. I got no reply. No one did. No one knew what his signature looked like. No one knew what *he* looked like. But Mandela's anonymity only made him more intriguing: a silent old man inspiring pop concerts and T-shirts. My knowledge of South African politics was patchy, but I felt the injustice of apartheid and twenty-seven years in prison as keenly as the next person.

And, like everyone else, my parents and I watched his release live on the BBC.

'There are those who will say to themselves, and try to remember, "Where was I on the day Nelson Mandela was released?"' blustered Jonathan Dimbleby.

In Pinner, I thought. With my parents. In the living room with the brown carpet.

'I think there'll be a civil war,' said Dad excitedly, pointing his camera at the TV set as we watched a crowd of people walk among cars at the entrance to Victor Verster prison.

'Can't you ever put that away?' asked my mother, disgust sitting on her lips. 'In twenty-four years of marriage I can count on my fingers the number of times I've seen your face without a camera attached to it. Are you really going to take a photograph of our television?'

'It's a historic moment,' explained my father, adjusting the lens.

Just then, the TV camera zoomed in on a man with white hair.

'There's Mr Mandela, Mr Nelson Mandela,' said the news reporter, with vibrato, 'a free man taking his first steps into a new South Africa.'

'And there's poor Winnie,' said Mum.

The three of us sat there in Pinner, crying with joy at the sight of this old man, hand in hand with his wife. We weren't completely sure what the whole thing meant for us personally, just as we hadn't been sure what kind of direct impact the fall of the Berlin Wall would have on the Andrusiers. But we knew we were alive at great, momentous times, when old notions of suppression were dying away. And then, there was something else: when Mandela lifted up his fist in a defiant salute, you couldn't think of him as a victim any more, only as a hero.

'The real question is,' said Dad, wagging a finger, 'what's he going to do next?'

§

In July of 1990, Nelson Mandela came to London to meet Margaret Thatcher, a staunch old ally of the Apartheid regime. He headed to Downing Street, mid-morning, and so did I.

'Can't sit for my portrait today,' I announced to my mother. 'I'm off to meet Mandela.'

My mother dropped me at Pinner station and offered her most encouraging smile.

'Have a good time,' she said. 'And don't be disappointed if it doesn't work out.'

'Don't worry, Mum. It'll work out.'

*

Downing Street was cordoned off. I got there just in time to see a flurry of distant flashes down by Number 10. The photographers traipsed back out to the main road, looking spent. A thought occurred to me.

'Do you know which hotel Mandela is staying at?'

'No idea,' said a scruffy journalist, carrying an enormous camera.

I asked the question again, several times, to the oncoming horde of newsmen. They all shrugged in succession.

Then one of them muttered, 'Park Lane Hotel, I think.'

'And where's that? Where's the nearest Tube?'

'Dunno. Probably Hyde Park Corner.'

So that was where I headed with my blank 5×8 card and biro.

It was obvious I had the right place because there were two ANC officials standing on the pavement.

'Is Nelson Mandela staying here?' I asked one of them.

'He is. But he's not here right now. Why do you want to know?'

'I want to get his autograph,' I explained.

The official was stocky and impatient-looking and began shaking his head. But the second official, who was younger and cheerier, overheard the exchange.

'If you want to wait inside,' he said, 'Mr Mandela should be here in about an hour.' He gestured for me to enter a lobby area to the right of the hotel's main entrance.

I stood patiently in the carpeted hall, the only autograph collector present, and readied myself for Mandela's greatness. I felt I'd entered a sacred inner sanctum. From my carpeted front hall in Pinner to here, and all I'd had to do was ask a photographer where he was staying! The hour felt like an Alvin hour – I was counting the squares on the wallpaper – but eventually there was a commotion on the pavement outside and a black Mercedes pulled up. The ANC officials rushed to open the car door, and out came Nelson and Winnie Mandela. They marched into the building and they and I were suddenly face to face.

'Can I have your autograph, please?'

'What is your name?' asked Nelson Mandela.

He looked tired and irritable, no suggestion of the Buddha smile from TV, nor the noble jawline. By the looks of him, he'd utterly got over the joy of being released from prison, and Winnie looked distracted too. Now I considered it, this couple looked about as happy as my parents. I wondered if maybe they'd had an argument? Perhaps Winnie and Maggie hadn't hit it off? Had Nelson eaten a bad prawn?

For a man this irritable, he was certainly taking his time over the autograph. He wrote out a long message on my card in big rounded handwriting.

To Adam, with compliments and best wishes, Nelson Mandela

He added the date, then handed the card to his wife without catching her eye, and she seemed to know the drill. She added her name above her husband's, then gave me a perfunctory nod. There. I'd done it. I'd had my audience with the Mandelas. I wasn't sure who'd had the bigger day – Nelson or me. But he clearly had the longer evening ahead of him. Winnie's patience was definitely running thin. 'Twenty-seven years I waited for you, Nelson,' I imagined her shouting from the hotel bath, 'and you treat me like one of your secretaries. It's all about you. First, you're physically absent, next emotionally. There's only so much loneliness a woman can put up with.'

By the time I got to the Tube, the early edition of the *Evening Standard* was out, and there was Mandela on the front cover, shaking hands with Maggie, displaying that big smile of his. 'Yeah, but his wife can't stand him,' I kept wanting to tell strangers on the journey home. 'Take it from me.' I gazed at the autographs I'd obtained, at the handwriting I'd captured on my blank card, with the historic date. I'll never sell it, I thought. Never. Before long, Mandela's frosty mood faded away completely, and by the time I was back in Pinner my anecdote was fully honed. Mine was a story about greatness, about triumph against all the odds.

'You didn't,' said my mum when I got into her car at Pinner station. 'I don't believe it.'

§

It turned out that Rachel couldn't stand me.

'You make me claustrophobic,' she complained down the phone. 'I'm not allowed other friends and you get jealous the whole time. I feel incredibly trapped. I'm too young to make this kind of commitment. It's all become too intense. We need a break. It's not you. I just need space to work out who I really am instead of being the person other people want me to be the whole time.'

I tried to reason with her, but she hung up. And now Alvin was answering the phone each time and telling me his daughter was in the bath or up the road with the dog, and could he pass on a message? I was hurt but also angry. If only I could be allowed to make my case, I could surely get Rachel to understand I had no interest in trapping her, that jealousy was a natural emotion, that couldn't she see – couldn't anyone – that the boys she called friends were really suitors in disguise?

'There's nothing you can do,' my mum said, when I explained what had happened, tears welling up in my eyes. 'You have to do as she asks. You have to back off and give her some space. With a bit of luck, she'll come back to you when she's ready.'

Sitting for my portrait again, my father watching *Mastermind* in the other room, shouting 'Government Communication Headquarters' at the television set, Mum seemingly oblivious to his voice. She had her look of reprieve again as she added tiny bits of clay to her son's face with the wooden tool. She lifted a finger to eye level and looked back and forth between the sculpture and the real thing. Then she took a deep breath and swivelled the portrait around to face me.

'So? What do you think?'

It was me, but not exactly. There was a certain look of determination around my portrait's eyes, as if I was expecting greatness in the near future. I wasn't sure that was how I felt now. And that smile playing on my lips? What was there to smile about so importantly? I pictured Rachel's family cracking open the wine, cracking up with laughter, someone rapping on the front door, a crowd descending – and me barred entry.

'I do like it,' I said. 'But I think you were right about the chin. There's a bit of an issue.'

RICHARD GERE

The reality is, we can change.
We can change ourselves.
We can change our minds.
We can change our hearts.
And therefore, the universe changes.

Richard Gere

It turned out there'd never been a time when my mother had felt beautiful. Even in her prime she'd been convinced she was heavy, out of place, peculiar-looking. This was down to the fact that her parents, Grandma Lotka and Grandpa Jožka, could always be counted on to find things to criticize.

'I don't remember them once saying I looked nice,' Mum mused. 'I suppose they didn't think I did. They had their minds on other things – starting a new life in England while dealing with incredible losses. But they did make some awful mistakes.'

'They should have made you feel beautiful,' I said. 'In your wedding photo, you look just like Audrey Hepburn.'

'Oh, I don't, Addie. You're sweet, but it's not true.'

It was a Friday evening, and my mother and I were talking at the dining table, as usual, at the back of the house. A pair of empty candlestick holders sat between us, the bent ones from Dad's childhood – bent, because Grandma Lily had once thrown them at her husband. The patio light was on, and my eye was caught by Mum's white stone carving to the side of the barbecue: a head emerging from rock, hands on chin, elbows stretching outwards like a person drawing breath.

'That was one of the things about your dad. When I first met him, he was always telling me how beautiful I was, always paying me such compliments. He never once criticized me. I couldn't believe anyone could find me that lovely.'

My mind wandered to Rachel, who had the new boyfriend with the bouffant hairdo and the self-regard. I'd seen him once at a party. Dan something. The idea of another boy kissing and touching her produced a stabbing pain in my stomach. As the pain subsided, I noticed it give way to cold hatred: hatred for Rachel, hatred for Dan Whatever, hatred for everyone. What did he have that I didn't? Was he handsomer? Was he suaver? I wasn't suave. Some leaves blew across the patio and brushed past Mum's sculpture, and I noticed an ennui take hold of me. Even if I hated Rachel, I knew it was her I wanted, not my mother. I wanted to be in the house in Preston Road, not this tribute house to my childhood, this museum.

I was actually glad when we heard the front door go, and Dad's voice called out, 'Lo-lo, I'm home! I've got a present for you.'

In swept Adrian and his curls and grey suit; he was dressed like a chauffeur. I watched him swagger through the living room, centre of gravity, purple Liberty bags dangling from his wrists. He stopped still, gave a triumphant smile and blinked effusively at my mother.

'*Another* present?' laughed Mum, patting her chest. She spun around, and her eyes lit up at Father Christmas before us. 'What have I done to deserve it?'

'You were just my Lo-lo Bo-bo,' said Dad. 'Come on. See if you like it. Sorry I'm late. My clients wouldn't stop talking. Now, guess what's on TV tonight? *Psycho!* We'll watch it, won't we?'

'I think I'll go and open my post,' I said, eyeing the pile on the kitchen work surface, wondering how my mother could keep falling for the man with the skin-deep charm. My father had stopped apologizing for the letter business by now, thank God, but it was still very much on my mind.

I felt it had smeared everything. It made my father's gifts seem like guilt offerings.

'My son! My son!'

Adrian reached out and stroked my cheek, too quickly for me to fully dodge.

'Oh no! My son's becoming stubbly! What happened to your cheeks, Doobs?'

'I guess they turned into these cheeks?' I said.

I picked up the post, featuring a large yellow envelope, postmarked Texas, and headed slowly up to my room.

'I hope you love the handbag,' I heard my father intoning as I went upstairs. 'Now, there are two sets of earrings to choose between. Take the ones you want. Up to you entirely. I'll give the other pair to my mother.'

'Your mother?'

While the party went on downstairs, I ripped open the large yellow envelope addressed to "Alan Andrewser" to find it contained an original painting of a skull and crossbones, accomplished by convicted serial killer John Wayne Gacy. This was sent courtesy of one Dwayne Patrick Jr, who'd enclosed a letter in babyish handwriting, suggesting I might like to either send him $350 for the "artwork" or return it. I'd read about Gacy, how he'd dressed as a clown, murdered dozens of young boys and buried them in his house. A strange artefact, for sure. I stared at the signature at the bottom right, in blood-red paint, and placed the monstrosity face down on my desk.

§

I'd not set eyes on Rachel for two weeks. Ever since she told me about the new boyfriend, I got a later train in the mornings, gliding into Preston Road at 8.25 a.m. instead of 8.15. I passed my eye across the crowd of strangers and pictured Rachel standing there just ten minutes earlier, her expression nondescript. She was excised from the scene now. The Tube swept up the passengers and on it journeyed. My mind was agitated. The Caribbean ticket-woman at Finchley Road, with the ever-changing hair – Coxy – would say, 'Ah, you missed Rachel! She came through already.' And I nodded and offered a tight smile, thinly disguising my desolation. I was a civilian now. I'd lost my lustre. Every step of the walk along Finchley Road – I'd done it so many times, I knew it bodily – was heavy and torturous. It was as if I was seeing all the greyness with new eyes now. What was the point of anything? My whole life had turned out to be a trick.

Most days after school I busied myself with lists of the famous; the American dealers' catalogues. They were identical, yet different. Same celebrities, same categories – signed photos/letters/signatures/signed documents – but each dealer had his own special twist. Some specialized in music or film, and some took more time over their descriptions than others. Occasionally, an expensively produced catalogue would arrive from one of the high-end manuscript dealers in London or New York, with the name of the dealer emblazoned on the front in gold or silver. These featured historical items with long descriptions and eye-watering price tags. I flicked through for the thrill, nothing more; letters of Einstein and Darwin impossibly beyond my reach.

I found myself going over everything that had recently happened with a killer's attention to detail. I spooled through the things Rachel and I had said to each other, the promises we'd made. I bunched together, categorized and recategorized my grievances with a peculiar glee, as if a cruel reordering of events might lead, paradoxically, to the recovery of everything good. Of course, it didn't. And so, when I inventoried what I remembered of Rachel's parents – the gaggle of pets, the discarded bottle openers, the idiosyncratic turns of phrase – I tried my best to dismiss them as a tinpot family that I was better off without; rejection, the privilege of the rejected. Then I returned to my dealers' lists, circled items of interest with a red pen and added messy asterisks along the side.

I was practising the piano furiously. I'd found out about a piano duet version of *The Rite of Spring* and was determined to master it. Stravinsky had written this version before his famous orchestration. There was a story of him romping through it, side by side with Debussy, somewhere in the French countryside. I made contact with a boy who'd left my school a few years earlier – Tom Adès – a fiendishly good pianist. 'Oh, he'll go far,' teachers always said about him. 'Phenomenal talent. A prodigy.' I sent him a letter at King's College, Cambridge, where I'd also applied to study music, asking if he'd consider performing the duet with me at school. To my surprise, he replied that he would, and we scheduled three rehearsals and a performance date. Tom would take the lower part, and I'd take the upper, if that was OK with me? I practised like crazy, slowing down the scatter gun, shrill runs at the top of the piano until I'd evened out the notes. I practised in different rhythms and at different speeds, and every now and then Rachel's new boyfriend would float into mind, and I'd be hammering his face, skewering it, beating him to a pulp with Stravinsky. Tom and I had our first rehearsal, and he was charming, complimentary, self-effacing. He played the lower part with astonishing skill and virtuosity, but still had the grace to say, 'Gosh, Adam – brilliant – how did you do that bit?'

§

The Inkwell held two autograph fairs per year at a hotel in Mayfair, and I went along with my father to browse the stocks of the dozen or so dealers who exhibited. The organizer was an absent-minded man in his seventies who trailed cigarette ash and seemed always in the middle of doing something else. Someone told me he'd once been a professional ice skater, which explained the way he slid around the carpet. The other dealers ranged from lovable rogues selling modern signed 8×10s of Kim Basinger and the like to suited business types selling Arthur Rackham illustrated letters, fingering Coutts chequebooks. I was the youngest collector there, at seventeen years old, which drew attitudes of kindness and derision in equal measure. Each dealer had only two chairs at his stall. The high-end ones grimaced when I perched on one. I was hardly going to spend much money.

'I don't suppose you have any murderers?' came an operatic voice over my shoulder.

'Murderers? No, I'm afraid not,' muttered the dealer. 'I had a Lord Lucan, but it sold.'

I took my opportunity.

'Might you be interested in a painting by John Wayne Gacy?' I asked, swivelling around in my seat to be confronted by a slender man with a large bald head and horn-rimmed spectacles. He was wearing a beige turtleneck jumper.

'I might be,' he boomed, 'although there are rather a lot of them about.' He was well spoken and his voice smooth like milkshake. He projected himself at quite an embarrassing volume.

'It's a really nice one,' I assured him.

'Come and see me at the Electric Ballroom one Saturday,' instructed the man. 'I'm Movie Guy.' He produced a business card, featuring a composite image of Bruce Lee and Elvis engaged in a discreet tête-à-tête.

'I'll bring it down,' I said.

'Excellent. I very much look forward to that.'

The following Saturday, there I was on Camden High Street carrying the John Wayne Gacy artwork in a padded envelope. I made my way into the venue, then through a dingy, tight warren of antiques stalls where hunched men were rifling through boxes of photographs. I felt weighed down by my secret serial-killer art. If people knew what I had on me! Eventually I found a tidily furnished stall, collector's albums laid out in a neat line, manned by Movie Guy. He was in mid-patter with another customer, an American tourist holding his jaw tightly, as if it might otherwise drop off.

'It depends what you're looking for,' said Movie Guy, his bald head lit from above and glistening. He was wearing a black turtleneck this time and white jeans. 'I have a nice Warhol print of the Electric Chair back at home, which is signed. Or, are you interested in Hitler?'

'Hitler? Ooh. What have you got?' asked the American gentleman. 'I could be interested.'

'I have a signed document,' said Movie Guy, flashing a smile and half closing his eyelids. 'Quite a nice example.' He picked up one of his folders, flicked past the first few pages, then held up the album. To the left was a photograph of Adolf Hitler staring angrily at the camera, to the right a piece of paper topped with a swastika, with a printed message in German above an illegible spidery black signature.

'Is that really his autograph?' I asked, screwing up my eyes with professional interest.

I'd never owned a Hitler. The idea of buying one was appalling and self-injurious, yet also somehow quite electrifying, like the forbidden thrill of the Chamber of Horrors at Madame Tussauds. There were odd times when I was tempted to pursue the feeling further, see what it would be like to buy my very own Führer. My father's face always intervened at such moments, frowning at my evil intent, a judge poised to pass the harshest of sentences.

'It's not an Autopen, if that's what you're worried about,' said Movie Guy. 'I've also got a nice signed photograph.' The dealer bent down and rummaged inside a plastic bag under his table, then withdrew a postcard-size photograph of the dictator, posing side on, his eyes concentrated into a shark-like glare.

'And how much are they?' asked the American.

'The document's a thousand, and the photo's fifteen hundred.'

'Nice. Very nice,' said the American. 'I'll think about it, but I'm definitely interested. I'll have a look at your books.' Movie Guy's face was stony, drained suddenly of its earlier enthusiasm.

'By all means. Be my guest.' Movie Guy closed the album against his chest and inclined his head slightly. A smile flickered on his lips then disappeared, as if he was finding it difficult to appear cheerful. Then he turned his attention to my padded envelope. 'Is that the Gacy, then?'

'It is. Take a look.'

I sheepishly handed over the goods.

Movie Guy tilted the skull and crossbones in his hands and touched some of Gacy's brushstrokes, presumably examining the murderer's chiaroscuro and tonal gradation. Meanwhile, I picked up a binder labelled 'Notorious and Undesirables' and started flicking through.

'The letters at the front are from Peter Sutcliffe,' muttered Movie Guy, rearranging his spectacles and lowering his voice a touch.

'You mean the Yorkshire Ripper?'

'Yes. He writes to my girlfriend from prison. The cards are fifty pounds each. The letters, a hundred.'

The notes were in frilly handwriting and signed 'Pete' with kisses; mostly Christmas and birthday cards – really quite charming, thoughtful notes. I turned the page.

'And that's Dennis Nilsen. The chap who killed for company. There's also a rare Jeffrey Dahmer letter there – take a look – the one who ate his victims and kept their body parts.'

I turned the pages. A cheque signed by Charles Manson, a signature of Fred West, witnessed by his arresting police officer, the marvellous Jeffrey Dahmer letter ('best wishes, Jeff') and a scribbled self-portrait by Mark David Chapman.

'He's the one who killed John Lennon,' explained Movie Guy, 'right after he got his autograph on his *Double Fantasy* album. Oh, and there are two really rare letters in there from Ian Brady, the Moors murderer.'

I'd seen a documentary about Brady's kidnapping and torturing of children. Here was a polite, long letter in carefully bunched-together handwriting, the gist being that Brady was really quite keen to get hold of a DVD of *Pretty Woman*. It was starting to become clear to me that serial killers were basically nice guys in unfortunate situations.

'He wants to watch *Pretty Woman*?' I asked.

'No accounting for taste,' giggled Movie Guy.

'So, how exactly did you get into murderers, then?'

'Oh, I've always liked things that are a bit . . . different,' explained Movie Guy, proffering a wide smile.

'Your girlfriend sends letters to the Yorkshire Ripper?'

'Well, he only replies to women is the problem. He phoned our house once – you wouldn't believe how innocuous he sounded. High-pitched northern accent.' Movie Guy's face crumpled into an odd smile, then the smile receded again. 'Now, the only problem I have with your Gacy – and it's very nice, don't get me wrong – is that I can only really sell paintings of his Pogo the Clown. That's what people want, you see. The clown.'

'You mean the clown he dressed up as for children's parties, before killing all the children?'

'Yes, exactly. Or I could probably use one of his Seven Dwarfs paintings, but they do have to be carrying their pick-axes.'

§

I'd recently been subscribing to a syndicate edition of *Celebrity Services Inc.*, a bulletin used mostly by journalists, which proved extremely useful for in-person autograph collectors like me. It told you exactly which celebrities would be arriving in London and where they'd be staying – sometimes it even published their flight numbers. I was sharing it with Yogesh Gupta and Darren Pendle.

It turned out that Richard Gere would be attending an exhibition of Buddhist art at the Royal Academy. As a devoted follower of the Dalai Lama, Gere had donated generously to the display. I was no big fan of Gere myself and didn't especially want his autograph; still, I turned up armed with a postcard photo of a debonair-looking Gere in a suit, back to back with Julia Roberts in her tiny miniskirt and leather boots. If I got that signed, I could get £40 or £50 for it. I stalked around outside the main entrance, alongside a couple of cameramen, while inside two Buddhist monks waited patiently in orange robes. A car swung into the Royal Academy's courtyard, and a smirking Richard Gere emerged, looking athletic and healthy. He stood still for a moment, surveying the scene, blinking and smiling like the lord of the manor.

'Mr Gere. Could you please sign this?'

He gave me his squiggle but didn't look at me. His eye was on the camera behind. Then he marched inside and threw his arms around the two monks in turn. The cameras flashed and Gere clasped his hands together in humility, never losing track of where the photographers were positioned. He took a step back for his assistant to present the monks with some neatly wrapped presents. Gere and the monks bowed at one another.

'The guy's an actor!' I wanted to yell. 'Don't fall for his gifts!'

Then I wandered into the lobby to have a go with a blank white card. Why not get two things signed? I could sell the second to Yogesh Gupta. But Gere was impatient now. He signed my card, but it was essentially just an "R" inside a big circle. I stood back to take it all in. Gere's smile was tight as anything; I imagined the morning facial exercises required to maintain it. His hair looked good; I couldn't take that away from him. He turned his head to the camera, then to a young female representative of the art gallery – she bowed her head and blushed – then back to the monks. He opened his arms wide as if to say, 'So, I guess this is me.'

§

It was the day of my performance of *The Rite of Spring* with Tom Adès. I'd plastered the school with advertisements, and the main hall was jammed. My family were there, and teachers were leaning down from the balconies above. I spotted Rachel's face in the audience. Who had told her about this?

I played the odd opening folk melody with my right hand, then Tom came in and between us we crept through the lugubrious first section. We got to the forceful bitonal chords with the wrong-footing rhythm – Tom hammered those, while I made spiky, shrill, stabbing interventions. Every few minutes, I found Rachel's face, then looked back down at the keyboard. I liked seeing where she was located and imagining how I might look from where she sat. 'Could Dan Shithead do this?' I wanted to shout. 'Or can he only do his hair?'

We reached the final section of Part One. Tom and I had our hands entwined, meaning that Tom's left hand was down at the bottom of the keyboard, playing in quavers, while his right hand was towards the top, playing in triplets. I was in the middle with both of my hands, playing fast semi-quavers, a third apart. The whole thing was an intense murderous mesh of sound. It was chaos, actually; controlled chaos. And then the final chords were unleashed, like the Hitchcock shower scene. I struck them with both hands – on beat, off beat – and we finished the job. We lifted our hands clean up and away from the keyboard.

§

Back in my bedroom, re-reading the new letter from Rachel. Things hadn't worked out with Dan. She'd never really loved him. She wasn't sure where to go from here, but she knew she definitely wanted me back in her life. She couldn't believe how amazing my performance of *The Rite of Spring* had been. It gave her a weird feeling, seeing me play like that, with all that energy and confidence. It got her remembering the times we'd spent together, and how much they'd meant. She'd been looking at all the silly presents I'd given her and was feeling soppy. Maybe, some day, I'd consider a conversation at the weekend – maybe even at her house this Saturday?

I smiled to myself and blinked while I manhandled the Gacy skull and crossbones back into the padded envelope.

'Not my kind of thing,' I'd explain in my note to Dwayne. 'Not really into serial killers these days. But if you do get hold of a Pogo the Clown painting, let me know. I may have someone for it.'

BORIS YELTSIN

You can build a throne with bayonets,
but you can't sit on it for long.

Boris Yeltsin

I achieved my A-level grades for Cambridge, and brought the Andrusier family crashing down to its knees. It was akin to my being declared a new member of the royal family; I let them bow and scrape.

'My son, the Cambridge student,' crowed my father, tearing up.

'A k'nacker,' said Grandpa Jožka, squeezing my cheek.

'Lucky boy,' said my mother.

'Lucky? Well, I did study,' I replied. 'Maybe luck isn't the right word?'

But that wasn't what she meant. She just wished *she* was going off to study; using her excellent brain again, setting off to explore.

Despite my own joy at the news, the fast-assembling marble statue of myself in my mind, complete with sceptre and laurel wreath, smiled uneasily, twisting its hands into an open question. Because I was contending with an unplanned gap year now. King's College's offer had stipulated a place deferred until 1993. So, I had to find something to do. And not just that. In just a few months' time, I'd be surrendering my girlfriend to an art history degree in Manchester.

I waved away my mixed fortunes. I was bolstered by success. A long-distance relationship wasn't going to be rocket science. Besides, before we got to that point on the distant horizon, there was a whole lot of pleasure in the foreground: for instance, the summer holiday Rachel and I had planned in the South of France.

'It's not appropriate, the two of you sharing a room,' my mother said, knitting her brow.

This was at my grandparents' house while we feasted on knedlíčky, the little Czech dumplings. Bowls of cinnamon, melted butter, chocolate powder, lemon juice, chopped nuts and soured cream were dotted around the floral tablecloth like little ideas. My grandfather had his special look of concentration, as if there might be important information inside the dumplings requiring his attention.

'It's cheaper if we share,' I tried.

'That may be,' said Mum, 'but I don't approve.'

'On the other hand, bobki,' said Grandpa Jožka, turning to Mum – he used his thumbs and index fingers to carefully place his cutlery horizontally across his plate – 'you can do the exact same thing in two rooms that you can do in one.' He chuckled to himself, then opened his arms into a shrug.

That was it. It was decided.

§

Our week-long holiday in Bandol, the town where D. H. Lawrence once rented a holiday home, came around. When I collected Rachel from the house in Preston Road, her mother, Maureen, took me to one side.

'Now, you will take care of her, won't you?'

She bundled an armful of condoms into my chest. I offered my most humble smile and nodded furiously, backing away towards the taxi.

Rachel and I frolicked in the sea, made love, had sex. We took a boat out to the little island of Bendor, where we ate steak frites at the cheapest restaurant we could find. We skinny-dipped. We quaffed warm wine. We turned pages of books without reading the words. Our hotel was a crappy three-star place that backed onto a busy bay blasted by sunlight, and we loved everything. We slapped suncream on each other's backs, we wore shades and laid out on towels like actors, we touched hands as we absorbed the heat from the sun above and the sand beneath. In the evenings, I struck naked poses in our bedroom – not even the laurel wreath – and Rachel sketched me with great seriousness.

There was a day when I counted my money on the hotel balcony, and it got blown clean out of my hands by a freak gust of wind.

'Oh shit! No! Look!' shrieked Rachel.

The notes flew up and over the top of the hotel as if being pulled by an invisible thread, and the two of us ran outside helplessly. We got there just in time to watch a few distant banknotes tumble down the end of the street and turn a corner. We stood laughing in the road, holding onto the stitches in our bellies. Who needed money? So, we'd eat less. Half a steak frites! We had love! We were invulnerable! We kissed at sundown, neither one of us mentioning what lay ahead: the fork in the road where Manchester began and life as we knew it ended. We sent our destiny packing, refused its clutches. That summer we were about the present moment, about what was in front of our noses. We cavorted and merged like the vibrant, colourful figures of a Dufy painting.

§

Three weeks into her first term at Manchester University and Rachel called to say things weren't working out the way she'd hoped. A long-distance relationship was proving too difficult.

She needed more intensity. She couldn't bear feeling so torn between her new life in Manchester and her old life with me. She needed to find out who she was. Oh, and she had a new boyfriend.

§

I began my twelve months' hard labour with a stint at Debenhams' toy department in Harrow. Character building, I told myself. It was a part-time Christmas job due to last until the end of December.

Before being let loose on the public, our team of workers was forced to sit through hours-long videos about the history of the store. Our instructor was a skeletal South African who leant into his sentences with great seriousness, as if the prosperity of a small impoverished nation might depend on the quality of our shelf stacking. We learnt how to deliver the Debenhams difference; how to spot shoplifting; how to potentialize with the merchandise. Breaks were spent in the smoky cafeteria on the top floor, where the full-time workers secluded themselves in a corner examining calluses, trading outrageous stories of wrongful dismissal. 'They pretend to pay us, and we pretend to work,' I heard one of them say, adding a raw cackle. I was strangely electrified by the dreary atmosphere up there, by the naked reality of it all. The bad food, the dim lights, the being in it all together, helped expunge thoughts of Rachel and sunsets in Bandol. I gossiped with co-workers, picked my nails, inhaled Cornish pasties, never daring to mention my love of classical music or the Cambridge degree that awaited me. I watched the cigarette butts multiply in the cafeteria's industrial-size communal ashtrays and mulled over my previous identity –

pianist, boyfriend, son, grandson – all stubbed out now; all
thrown into the mix.

My first task on the shop floor was to stack a long shelf
with toy trolls. These were all the rage in 1992: little monkey-
faced things with huge, spiky, brightly coloured hairdos. I
lined them up painstakingly, one ugly mug next to the other.
At 9.30 a.m. the doors flew open and within thirty seconds a
gang of seven-year-olds had swept their arms along the shelf
and sent my troll community into a mini-apocalypse. The
gang moved on, and I was instructed by my department head
to restack the shelf immediately. I complied, but it was only a
matter of minutes till the next attack. Meanwhile, a concession paper aeroplane display started up near the main till.
'Three in a pack, they all come back,' bellowed the operator
as he threw the cardboard things around in circles. Gangly,
gnarly faced toddlers marched in every direction, their
exhausted-looking parents lagging behind, traipsing buggies.
Someone switched the background music to deafening
volume: 'All I want for Christmaaaas is youuu'.

With most of my friends away at university, I made the
best of my co-workers, presenting myself as a mysterious,
sagely comic figure. I had a failed drink with a softly spoken
long-haired goth who'd never heard of John Major (the
prime minister). I offered trite advice to an Asian girl trapped
in an arranged marriage (You have to leave him. You owe it
to yourself). I attended the Debenhams Christmas party,
which featured a cabaret focused almost exclusively on the
art of cross-dressing, our department manager channelling
Diana Ross doing 'Upside Down'. I rang the tills, stacked the
trolls, I wished – I *prayed* – for a juicy shoplifting incident. I
told anyone who listened for long enough about the tragedy

of my ex-girlfriend in Manchester; how she'd dumped me for another bloke, but hey ho, what can you do?

'That's bad,' said a forceful, po-faced co-worker named Donna. 'Did I tell you what I did when my boyfriend left me? I went round his house and smashed all his windows.'

In the evenings, I met with the few remaining schoolfriends still in town. We commiserated with one another over our lacklustre existences, the challenge of being stuck home with parents. My father nowadays had the permanent frantic look of a man on the run. His only conversation was "work stress" and he paced around like a caged lion, as if it was him being held against his will in Pinner, rather than me. Still, I was conscious that my continued presence in the family home had the effect of holding things in place – just about. With my sister gone two years earlier, we'd reconfigured the family shape to something workable, essentially with me installed as my mother's replacement husband. That arrangement was starting to fray at the edges now that I was in deep mourning for Rachel. It was hard to imagine how this might play out once I'd gone to Cambridge. Surely the fracture lines I was guarding would finally break, and my parents would drift like icebergs in opposite directions.

'Don't sweat it,' said my friend Steve. 'It's not your problem. Look, why don't we go travelling together. May till July? Be fun.'

'Sure. Let's do it. But where would we go?'

'Dunno. Somewhere weird,' said Steve. 'Anywhere you like.'

'Let's see.' I racked my brains for the remotest places I could think of. I pictured languages written right to left, mountain ranges shrouded in cloud. 'China? Shall we go to China?' I suggested.

'China? Sure. Fuck it.'

My next job was in the lettings department of a Muswell Hill estate agent. The boss was a nasty older man with a beard, conducting an open affair with the married co-boss, a woman in her forties named Devika; she wore a sari. At half-term, she brought her children in to play on the photocopy machine while she waltzed in and out of the boss's office, slamming the door behind her. When the boss was in there alone, he teased the door open so his staff could overhear his insulting phone calls.

'Could I speak to someone with half a brain, please?' he'd say.

The boss didn't know who I was and never spoke to me, for which I was glad. If I found myself in his field of vision, I surely stood out no more than the fax machine. No such luck for the other employees, who had to endure his sexist jokes, lingering eye and accompanying paltry pay cheques. I shared a room with a self-effacing single mother with a mournful laugh – Deedee. She hated her job and had dreams of doing worthwhile things; further education, for a start, and then maybe set up her own company some day. She made sad phone calls to her ex, pleading with him to pay up money for their ten-year-old son.

'Useless,' she'd say, putting the receiver down, shaking her head with well-worn disappointment. 'He won't take any responsibility. He only thinks about himself. He thinks this is all funny.'

I made it my challenge to amuse Deedee, bring her some

joy. I'd practised enough with my mother, and it wasn't hard. I made jokes about the boss, about his horrible affair with Devika. I made Deedee laugh out loud about the state of my parents' marriage, about Rachel dumping me, about people in general.

'It's all a big nothing,' I concluded, wise old office boy that I was. 'People basically stink.'

'Oh don't, don't!' Deedee would shriek, clapping her hand over her mouth.

'You should leave this job,' I instructed. 'You're better than this. You deserve better.'

'Do I?'

'After this stint as an office boy,' I waxed, 'I'll never work for another soul again. Who knows what I'll end up doing, but it'll never involve putting on a suit. I'll work for myself. I'll be free. Life's too short.'

Deedee looked encouraged by my youthful energy and wild eyes.

'You're right,' she said, goading herself on with a fierce nod. 'And one day, I'll do the same thing. No doubt about it.'

I had my own car now: a two-tone Nissan Laurel that had belonged to my grandfather's brother, Uncle Marek, who no longer drove. It was wide and low, like an American car. I careered up and down the A406 to get to work each day, blasting jazz through the speakers – late, edgy, funky Miles or sighing, world-weary Billie Holiday. My mind was a blank, in a white rage. I felt like a soldier going into battle. A member of London's workforce, an automaton. How had it come to this? Rachel would slide into my thoughts the same way Greta Garbo used to, as an untouchable film star, a mythical figure, as someone living in a parallel universe, and I'd find myself smiling cruelly as if I should have known this would end up happening, as if I must be misremembering the better times.

Sometimes, racing home after work, the thought crossed my mind that I could turn my Nissan off the road entirely. Yes, a possibility. Death was a mere second or two away; perhaps I'd twist the steering wheel and be done with it? It was nothing more thought through than that. I felt utterly calm. My life didn't rush before my eyes. In fact, I drifted easily towards the idea, as if closing my eyes to fall into a dream. At the crucial moment, something intervened. I woke myself up, wrested control. I wasn't going to give in, I decided. I'd rise above all this, take my situation in the stranglehold it deserved.

§

When I heard that Boris Yeltsin was in London, I pulled an immediate sickie. Yeltsin's autograph was rare, in the £300 to £400 bracket. You couldn't get him through the post. The only examples I'd seen had been in German mail-order auctions. I used to pore over those little illustrated catalogues for hours, back then, adding asterisks and fantasizing about what I could own. Thanks to the money I made from selling duplicates to pen pals, I could sometimes afford to send in bids, and I even occasionally got things, like a rare signed photo of the jazz pianist Bill Evans. When it arrived, I moved a few celebrities around in my collector's album, removed some lesser individual, and squeezed Evans in. I had several hundred autographs now, which I examined, touched, admired regularly. I gazed at my gamut of treasures – from

Clint Eastwood to Bill Evans to Mother Teresa – with the pride of a museum curator. My collection: a microcosm of world events, uniquely tailored by me.

But I didn't have Yeltsin, and I wanted him.

'Migraine,' I explained to Devika.

'Well, make sure you're back at work tomorrow,' came the stony reply.

I scoured the newspapers until I found a mention of the hotel where the Russian leader was staying – the Hyde Park Hotel in Knightsbridge – then I headed there with my cards and a pen. I felt this was Mandela all over again, a return to my former greatness. I had a spring in my step.

With the front of the hotel cordoned off by police, I headed to the back entrance. A red flag with hammer and sickle hung above the door, and a matching red carpet ran from the hotel building out to the pavement, where plain-clothes officers in shades talked into headsets; KGB, by the looks of their knobbly features. I hardly needed to ask if Mr Yeltsin was staying here – it was self-evident – and there were no other collectors around, so I fancied my chances. I brought to mind my previous autograph escapades, of Miles Davis and Ray Charles, that period before stacking trolls and filing lettings contracts, when life made better sense.

A commotion at the back as three agents ran towards the hotel along the edge of Hyde Park. Then, in a matter of moments, a great entourage of motorcycles rushed towards the hotel behind them, followed by a dozen black limousines. This was it. Yeltsin arriving. The cars all pulled into the kerb at the exact same moment, and out of them streamed at least a hundred men in suits. Some walked, others jogged, all heading towards the hotel's back entrance. One KGB officer assigned himself to me alone and marked my every move.

'I only want an autograph!' I exclaimed.

And then I saw him. Or rather, it: Yeltsin's white hair, sprayed rock-hard, unwavering in the breeze. The Russian leader pounded the pavement like a bear, his fists raised in the air, a wild drunk making one last important point before being dragged to bed.

'Mr Yeltsin!' I called out. 'Could I have your autograph?'

And I saw his head jerk in my direction. He'd definitely heard me. Then he let rip what could only be described as a long and doleful grunt. I took it as a firm 'No'. But there was something more in it. Was the poor statesman struggling under the psychic weight of his responsibilities to Mother Russia? Was he reaching out to me in brotherhood? Either way, his white hair bobbed past like a pacesetter at a horse race, and the entire security detail crammed into the hotel behind him.

It was over. How depressing. This wasn't the heyday. It was an unqualified failure. And now it was raining. I began sloping back towards the Tube, but then I spotted another black limousine cruising slowly towards the hotel's back entrance. That seemed interesting. It came to a halt, and who should emerge, looking flustered? Only Norma Major herself, the prime minister's wife, the Patron Saint of Normal. I asked her for an autograph. It would have been rude not to.

'Oh yes, of course,' she said, and she wrote, 'Norma Major' on my card. As she handed it back, the rain picked up and she smudged her signature with her thumb.

I thanked her the way you might thank someone for sneaking ahead of you into a parking place, and thought, Yep, that's about right. Whisk yourself off to Pinner to spend another Norma No-Mates evening with your beloved parents.

§

Smiling into the sunlight on the China Sea, reading the opening lines of *David Copperfield*:

'Whether I shall turn out to be the hero of my own life, or whether that station will be held by anybody else, these pages must show . . .'

A monsoon was forecast, but the skies were clear. No one knew I was here, right now, on the deck of this four-day ferry from Shanghai to Hong Kong – such pleasure in that. No one except Steve, of course, who was sat beside me sunning his face and complaining about the lack of snacks. We'd bought "VIP" tickets for this trip, but that hadn't stopped them closing down the main bar on day two. All our special tickets actually meant was that we got double portions of the same food they slopped out for the Chinese passengers. Dumplings of Unknown Meaty Substance in a soup of Unknown Liquid. What I'd have given for some knedlíčky!

The sun disappeared quite suddenly into cloud, and the boat rocked heavily to one side before righting itself again – perhaps that monsoon was on its way now. I imagined my parents in the living room at home sharing a thought about their son, wondering where on earth I might be, then looking back in different directions. On a boat in the South China Sea, reading Dickens. Who'd have thought it?

As the boat swayed, I recalled our 7,000-step walk up Mount Tai An. According to folklore, you'd live to a hundred if you made it to the top. I was happy enough with nineteen. I thought of the jazz band at the Peace Hotel in

Shanghai; elderly men striking noble Louis Armstrong poses, while the Japanese businessmen at the next table fell into alcohol-induced hysteria. I remembered how drunk Steve and I had been at the snooker club in Beijing – a bottle of vodka each, and telling the guy playing the keyboard that I was Elizabeth Taylor's son and his believing me. I brought to mind the panoramic view at the top of Moon Hill in Yangshuo, the limestone peaks stretching into the distance like a background painting to an episode of *Monkey*. Yes, there was no doubt I was on the world stage now, and I'd made it through a horrible year. Debenhams, estate agents, Norma Major; I patted my chest where a badge of ordinariness ought surely to be positioned. What doesn't kill you makes you stronger. Hadn't someone once said that?

STEVE REICH

I discovered that the most interesting music of all was made by simply lining the loops in unison, and letting them slowly shift out of phase with each other.

Steve Reich

Day one at Cambridge University. My parents sped off in the Volvo towards their uncertain future, while I headed into the town centre to buy a bottle of whisky. I was dressed in tie-dye trousers, Converse boots and a Chairman Mao cap. A hypnotic yellow bead swayed in the centre of my forehead. I popped into Athena to buy posters, then on to Sainsbury's for the whisky. I had no idea why whisky – hated the stuff. Anyway, I managed to drop it right in the middle of King's Parade. It smashed into a thousand pieces, a cloud of tarry, alcoholic fumes lifting up off the road. I did my best to look nonchalant, keep on walking. An act of disdain. Nothing to see here! I narrowed my eyes in the midday sun.

Minimalist music blared through my speakers as I decorated my college bedroom. The kind of stuff I was into these days was a preacher shouting the phrase 'It's gonna rain' for seven whole minutes on a loop – two recordings of the same voice overlapping till the phrase utterly lost its meaning. I put on Steve Reich's *Drumming*, volume at full pelt; the hollow taps of African rhythm at the start. While it gained its forward momentum, I Blu-tacked up postcards taken from my drawers at home: stills from Buñuel's *Un Chien Andalou* (I'd never seen it), a few Van Goghs, Che Guevara, and my photo of Frank Sinatra with the silver smudge. Then I set out my panoramic view from Moon Hill in China – twenty pictures taken in quick succession. I added photos of Grandpa Jožka in his army garb, staring out to sea through binoculars, my father dressed as a Hassid, my sister and me aged five and two, her fingers poised to pinch me. And I put up the posters I'd just bought at Athena: Escher's hands drawing each other, Dalí's landscape dotted with drooping clocks, Matisse's *Snail* – did I even like Matisse?

The music got to the bit where one of the drummers sped up, moved ahead of the other, made a dash to the next beat of the bar. I stopped still to take in the moment my ear could never quite grasp, the bit where the two speeds were in conflict, the beats of the drum toppling away like skittles while the accelerating drummer settled into his new position. Now the drummers were in sync again, but different – the new position in the bar opened up a different rhythmic exchange. I thought suddenly of my braces, years earlier, how my mother would drive me to Harpenden after school to get them tightened by the orthodontist; for several days my mouth felt wrong, like it belonged to someone else.

The xylophones entered now, against the rippling of drums, and Steve Reich did the same thing again; incorrigible. He made one of the xylophonists speed up and make a run for it, to get to the next beat in the bar. I delighted, again, in that moment of toppling, the blurring, the bit where the rhythm and tune broke apart. And I heard something else too, in the chaos: a kind of clicking sound made by the xylophone – part of its timbre. Like the shaking of dice in a closed fist. It had always been there but only now could I hear it. How was that?

I took a step back to digest this new collage of myself on the wall and touched and fiddled with my stud earring – left ear for straight men in 1993. That had been a nice touch in the closing weeks of summer; stick a hole in your ear and feel you've really done something.

'Only weak men wear earrings,' Adrian had adjudicated, shaking his head like King Solomon.

'Guess I must be weak, then.'

I'd smoked my first cigarettes that summer. A stale pack of abandoned Marlboro Reds taken from the dining-room sideboard, best before 1979, dry as old straw. My parents in bed, I secretly smoked out of my bedroom window, watched the veil of grey curl dispassionately around the side of the house, my mind vivid with possibility.

And now, in my college bedroom, I sparked up a Marlboro Light while *Drumming* reached its conclusion. All the elements in play in the grand finale, everything from earlier on joining in, all the rhythmic and harmonic gestures, all of life vibrating and pulsing like the sun's rays beating down on a boiling-hot summer's day.

§

Freshers' week was cacophonous. A circus. So many people. They mostly had the same face, these people. It took days to separate them. They were sparky and clever and nervous about the experience, none of them realizing that they – we – were the experience. I tried myself out on everyone, shuffled us all like a giant pack of cards. One minute, I was faux-discussing the Bloomsbury Group with a white-haired Provost, someone refilling my wine glass, attaching it to my plate with a plastic device. Next, clambering over the locked gate at the back of college with boys I'd just met – beery-breathed, heart racing. Now I was dragging on a joint with some bloke from Leeds and laughing like a child, laughing, weeping so much and not even knowing why. Not knowing who this guy *was*, actually. And then someone put on Aphex

Twin, and my ear was drawn to that, drawn fully deep down into that – underwater, by the sounds of it – another time, another place. In the college bar, puking into a toilet, thinking 'Armitage Shanks. Armitage Shanks' and picturing my mother's face. What would she think? She couldn't know, couldn't guess, how I was breaking away from the beat now, moving on to the next one. I felt a rush of guilt, then stared in the mirror, only half recognizing the blurred rubbery student peering back, and wondering, what do *I* think – what do *I* think of this drunk? My father's composite photos came to mind: Oliver Reed's face on Adam Andrusier's body. I laughed as the thought drifted away.

§

During the daytimes, I returned to the old me. I practised the piano like a madman; difficult pieces by composers I thought only I had discovered: Scriabin, Nancarrow, Suk, Sorabji. The time signatures changed each bar, the runs were at breakneck speed, concurrently, in both hands, the tunes wild and fragmented. The music I liked now sounded like psychosis, and that was when I was playing it right. I practised till my fingers hurt. I practised so much that the guy next door, Vaughan, changed to a room on the floor above. While I played, I thought about my performance of *The Rite of Spring*, with Rachel's face there in the audience, my family clapping.

And then Rachel was there. Actually right there. At the front of Garden Hostel. Alive, pretty, smiling uncertainly.

'Hi,' she said.

She'd come to Cambridge to see me, she explained. It had

been over a year now and she wanted to see how I was. So, we drank tea together in my college bedroom. I watched her eyes as they moved across the gap-year collage on my wall. I'd been everywhere, by the looks of it. I'd conquered the world. But then, so had she. There was an American boy-friend now. He had a name. They'd spent the summer in California together. I pictured them in Beverly Hills; at Universal Studios; on rides at Disneyland, water splashing in their faces. A cooler atmosphere descended. Still, I decided to walk my old girlfriend all the way to Cambridge station – for old times' sake. We hugged, then unlocked eyes. We each went back to our own life.

I returned to mine via an off-licence on Mill Road. During the twenty-minute walk back to college I drank an entire bottle of wine. When I got back to college – the bar hotting up, 8.30 on a Friday night – I was blind drunk.

A coincidence! Sitting in one of the booths was Rachel's ex: Dan with the bouffant hair. He was with a girl. It looked like a first date. I joined the pair with my snakebite and black. Delighted to meet you. Ever heard about me? I must have had a lot to say because Dan's face was ponderous, amused, concerned in alternation. The date looked impatient.

Now I was at the bar ordering myself multiple drinks, and my friends were restraining me, one on each side.

'You've had enough, mate,' the barman said.

I broke free from the armlock and fell prostrate to the bar floor. It caused a hush to descend. A circle of concerned faces appeared above me.

'I have no life,' I yelled, starting to weep.

In a packed college bar. At 10. On a Friday night.

'I have no life!'

They carried me to my room, the friends – two took legs, two took arms. When we got there someone put on music. More friends appeared. They laid me down on my bed, and I flipped my arms wide open; like Jesus on the cross, someone later observed. I writhed around, I puked into my dustbin, I made confused mutterings about Rachel and my empty life. Someone took off my trousers. Someone else put on the kettle. People made toast.

Next day, I awoke with my body punctured – airless and light. My head felt sledgehammered. I put on my tie-dye trousers and staggered into college. I phoned my sister in Durham from the porter's lodge payphone, revelled in the sympathetic singsong of her voice – 'poor you', 'don't worry', 'oh, darling' – Ruth, who never ever wanted upsetting things to happen to her little brother. Then I lurched into town. I found a barber, and in I went. There was only one thing for a situation like this: a haircut.

'I'll have a zero all over,' I demanded.

'You sure?'

'Never been surer. Take it all off.'

'And the bead? What do you want to do with that, mate?'

'You know what? The bead can go,' I declared. 'I'm done with it.'

§

One day, someone mentioned an "email", how a person they knew was sending one from the Turing Room. What was that, then? A message on a computer you could send to someone in America, they explained. I couldn't see why you'd bother. Why not just write them a letter, I asked, or phone them? Apparently, it was instantaneous – that was the

thing. I still didn't get it. America was in a completely different time zone. What was the point? I was certain it was a fad
that would pass.

Meanwhile, autographs were arriving in my college
pigeonhole in a steady stream. I retrieved them casually. Oh,
another Ronald and Nancy Reagan signed photo – Ronald
didn't sign if you wrote to him but try Nancy; *she'd* get him
to sign. A Schulz sketch of Snoopy. Finally! I couldn't work
out what I'd done right. The celebrities wrote from around
the world. But Steve Reich was still quiet – I'd requested a
musical quote from *Drumming*. I felt detached from this old
hobby of mine, felt its pull weakening. There was something
about autographs that didn't fit with the way I was changing
now. Whenever I remembered my silent collection sitting
in the same display folders in my bedroom in Pinner, I felt
constrained by the past, irritated by it. People collected to
keep things the same, I'd come to understand, or rather to
stay the same. I thought of the way my father talked about
his postcards; the repetitive old speech about continuity,
how his postcards made him feel like a rescuer, a witness.
Well, I didn't want to be a witness. I didn't want to stay the
same. I wanted a new narrative. I wanted to see who else
I could be.

§

One Sunday, I wandered into a community hall in Cambridge town centre, where a sale of bric-a-brac was taking
place. I was stunned to find a stall selling autographs. A man
of about sixty with a very straight neck and NHS glasses
stood there like a bird, his hands behind his back, occasionally bobbing forward to rearrange his binders. I stepped up

and flicked through, gliding past the signed photos of TV stars and modern-day heads of state; the very same poses Margaret Thatcher and François Mitterrand had sent me.

'I've a lot more at home,' interjected the man. His voice was velvety and operatic. His tongue perched pensively at the side of his mouth. 'Do you collect?'

'Well, I used to,' I explained, pulling my hands across my shaved head. 'These days, I mostly buy and sell.'

'Oh, you do, do you? So, what do you have for sale, then?' asked the man.

He took off his glasses and pinned his eyes open with appetite. Then he quickly closed them again in a tight squint, as if he knew better, remembered to defer his pleasure.

'Oh, I've got loads of stuff in my college room,' I said, shrugging.

'So, why don't I give you my telephone number? I live out at the edge of town. You can come and look through the rest of my collection any time you like. Now let me see . . .'

The man found a scrap of paper and scribbled down his address and phone number. He wrote his name, in capital letters: DAVID MOORCOCK.

§

A week later, and there I stood at a mossy front door, leaning on my bicycle, a binder of autograph duplicates dangling from my arm in a Sainsbury's bag, a hundred items priced from £5 to £100. I heaved at the brass knocker and noticed that the whole front facade of the house was covered in moss, akin to a man's face overgrown with hair, like the vegetation at the front of Ronnie Barker's house in Pinner when Adam Brichto and I had to stick our heads in a hedge to see through.

'How nice to see you again,' said the man, standing on his doorstep in a striped shirt, grey flannel trousers and sheepskin slippers. He struck a magnanimous pose there, his hands placed high up on his waist, around his ribs almost. 'Why don't you leave your bike at the front, and come on in?'

'Thanks.'

I followed him in through the front door.

'It's downstairs,' he said, holding a finger in the air and leading the way down a tight staircase into a cellar.

We were in a vast underground library that stretched way beyond the front door. The ceiling was low and the smell a musty mildew. It was very dark – you'd never have known it was 4 p.m. – just an occasional yellow tinge from sparse lighting overhead. The shelves were filled with old books and piles of papers. We walked for perhaps half a minute, through a tight corridor of bookshelves until a desk and two chairs appeared in a clearing.

'I built this basement for my collection,' explained Moorcock. 'Been collecting for forty-seven years, you see. Not everything's signed, mind. But this section here has all my letters from writers and artists.'

He gestured to three shelves of a bookcase, filled with binders labelled "Literature A–C" and the like. He wanted to show me. He wanted to show me his things.

'I spend a lot of time down here, these days,' he said, a mournful glint in his eye.

'So, you used to write off for autographs yourself?' I asked.

'Still do,' said Moorcock. 'Most of them I'm keeping, mind. But you never know. It depends what items *you've* got.' His eyes lingered on my plastic bag and his smile flicked suddenly off.

Like Movie Guy, I thought, remembering the bald man's effort to stay friendly while something else lurked beneath the surface. Place Moorcock in my old life, and he could play Movie Guy. These people were interchangeable. Or was he more like my dad? I thought of the collector's albums piled up in the study in Pinner, filled with things my father would never sell.

And then things became very blurry. Moorcock was in a seat, turning the pages of my binder ferociously, proprietorially. That was the drill, wasn't it? This was what we collectors did: we rifled through each other's things, never knowing what we were looking for till we found it. We used the same language, too. We talked about items and rarity. We talked about condition. He rubbed his chin and offered various grunts and coughs. A concentrated expression settled on his face, as if his life depended on whichever autograph he might today decide to acquire. Feel free to look through any of *my* books, I heard him say, and his voice was tinny, the acoustics of the basement robbing it of its earlier fruitiness.

Is there an ex-wife, I wondered? Estranged children? Some background tragedy keeping him down here in this basement, penning letters to David Hockney and Jasper Johns, arranging their responses in alphabetical order? I remembered my mother telling me about the terrible things Adrian witnessed as a child. His parents fighting, and the time his mother and grandmother yelled so much at his father that Adrian called the police. He was thirteen years old when that happened.

I wanted, suddenly, to be in the college bar. I wanted to be with the guy from Leeds with the foot-long joints; I wanted Aphex Twin. I wanted that particular flavour of wondering who I was, where things might lead. This here, this dungeon on the outskirts of town, was my old stomping ground – the bit I already knew about.

I'm not a collector, I wanted to shout. *I'm not like you!*

I imagined Moorcock holding me in his basement till I gave that idea up, till I agreed to calm down and be the old me. I imagined rapping my knuckles on a wooden trapdoor while the old man had his tea upstairs, watched the news, ate beans on toast, took his time over a crossword.

'Now, if there's anything you want from my albums,' said David Moorcock, pursing his lips and blinking, 'just take it out and put it to one side. Because I'd absolutely love your Paul McCartney.'

§

Back at college, an airmail envelope from America was sitting in my pigeonhole. Steve Reich had replied. In jagged handwriting he'd written out the first bars of *Drumming* as requested – the opening rhythmic gestures – the rudimentary cells that led to everything that came later. I was glad to receive it, but my palms didn't sweat, and I didn't stifle my pleasure the way Movie Guy or David Moorcock might have. Honestly, I didn't even think of it as an item. I Blu-tacked it to my wall.

Later, in my room practising the piano, my fingers careering around the keys like parts of a bigger machine, I felt myself becoming a stronger flavour of the new self I was building. You add to yourself, and keep on adding, I thought.

But did you have to incorporate the bits from before? Not consciously, you didn't. It was just there anyway. Nothing ever really went away. It all got recycled.

I lit up a cigarette and thought of my mother, how she was still installed in the house in Pinner. I felt a stab of guilt. No matter. Nothing to be done. I couldn't rescue her. Just focus on this cigarette, see where it leads you. I smoked so much, nowadays, I feared my lungs would pack up. Sometimes, at night, I opened an eye and thought of all the ones I'd already smoked, imagined them in a big pile in the middle of the room, wondered what my mother would think. My poor abandoned mother. I'd never wanted to abandon anyone, but perhaps you had no choice in the end. Once you started off in a direction, it had a momentum of its own. And I'd started. I knew I'd started.

SALMAN RUSHDIE

THE SATANIC VERSES

THE CONSORTIUM

It may be argued that the past is a country from which we have all emigrated, that its loss is part of our common humanity.

Salman Rushdie

During the summer of my first year at university, my grand-parents came to Pinner for supper. Uncle Marek was there – Grandpa's brother – and his wife, Ilse. My sister returned home from Durham for the occasion, and we blinked at each other in code, variously, at the things our parents said. I was dying for a cigarette, but that would have to wait till mid-night, out of the window of my old bedroom.

I'd walked everyone through the events of my first year at college, missing out the dramatic bits – the drink, the drugs, the parties – missing out that I'd become an entirely different person. When I told them about the rendezvous in David Moorcock's basement, Adrian made a comment about his entrepreneur son, and fancy finding an autograph dealer to trade with in Cambridge city centre. 'My son, the business-man,' he said. Then my grandfather got onto the subject of Uncle Marek's university days.

'I paid for it all, but he never worked,' he complained. 'The only thing my dear brother did was play tennis.'

Uncle Marek blushed and laughed and patted the table-cloth with both hands. 'Well, I was a good player,' he protested.

'Player, yes. Worker, no.'

'Oh, Daddy,' said my mother.

'What, bobki? What is it?'

'Nothing, nothing.'

The whole scene was so familiar, and yet not. It was like watching a long-running play I'd seen a thousand times before. I had been pretty sure these family members had compelling personalities. Now they read their lines, played their parts, like ham actors. Perhaps because things weren't changing for them any more. But for me it was different. I was inside the very act of changing. I knew I was the dynamic thing – a youth, a stripling – on whom old ideas were fast losing their grip. I felt like my own doppelgänger, sitting there at the dinner table nodding and smiling at these relatives as if we were back in sync again when I knew we weren't.

And then the topic of Grandpa's other brother came up – Aron. Aron, who was left behind in Czechoslovakia with Grandpa Jožka's parents in 1938.

'What was that story about him escaping?' I asked. 'Didn't he jump off a train?'

'Yes, well, we don't know for sure,' said my grandfather.

'We should find out somehow,' said Mum, 'shouldn't we?' She looked worried, suddenly.

I remembered us discussing this in the past, how I used to fantasize about finding Aron somewhere in Eastern Europe and reuniting him with his brothers after a half-century apart.

'But we *know* what happened,' piped up Uncle Marek, raising an eyebrow in disbelief, opening his palms. 'What are you talking about? How did you forget?'

'What? We know what, exactly?' asked Grandpa, fixing his brother with a stare.

'Well, when I was in Czech-o some years ago, I met a fellow who was in the same work camp as Aron. You know the story already, Jožka. So, this fellow, he organized an escape from the labour camp – successful, as it turned out – and he asked our brother to join him. Our brother refused. Aron refused. He didn't want to leave Mother behind.'

'Now *that*,' said my grandfather, 'I didn't know.'

'Ach, I told you already. You knew!' said Marek. 'They perished together.'

Everyone went quiet. I heard the distant caw of a crow in the garden.

'Well,' said Grandma Lotka, 'can I interest anyone in a nice piece of cheesecake?'

§

'What's it like being dead, then?' I asked the Ouija board, back at King's at the start of my second year. I had a new room, at the front of college, and a new group of London friends.

'B-O-R-I-N-G.'

'Are you happy, at least?'

'NO.'

'Is there anything to do?'

'NO.'

Our spirit-messenger was tired, as was Josh – he'd passed out on my bed. It was 3 a.m. and Jessie was drunk to the point of hallucination, her finger sliding off the glass. But Carrie and I were determined to keep going.

'Is there sex in the afterlife?'

'NO.'

'Are you there with any of your friends?'

'NO.

Since Uncle Marek had told the story about Aron, I'd been conducting these nightly séances. The whole day led towards the moment I laid out the letters around my coffee table. We started by asking the spirit its name. The one I always wanted was Aron Schwartzmann from Český Těšín; instead, we got Andy from Peru, Sue from Egypt and our current jokester: Bob from Peking.

'So, what's the meaning of life, Bob, in your humble opinion?'

Carrie stifled a yawn.

The wine glass hesitated, started circling, seemed cornered. Then it sprang into action.

'F-U-G-U-E-S.'

We fell about laughing. Because I had a fugue to write for the next day, didn't I. Because I always had a fugue to write. Either that, or piano variations in the style of Beethoven; or a chorale harmonized the way J. S. Bach liked it. My Cambridge degree had turned out to be about as dry as Ryvita. "Music" wasn't the name for it. "The Science of Music" would have been more accurate. If they'd given us lab coats, we students could have conducted experiments on what conceivable benefit to mankind a degree like ours could bring. Publish the results in the *Guardian*.

It was playing that kept me going. Playing, where my heart lay. To hell with lectures on sixteenth-century notation; I was going to perform Ravel's Piano Concerto in King's College Chapel if it was the last thing I did, and I was going to do it like a terrible motherfucker. No one asked me to, actually. I volunteered. I actively relished the prospect of performing to a crowd of five hundred at the end-of-term concert. The other music students would be there. My tutors would be there. If I was no good at harmonizing fugues using pen and paper, let them see what I could do on a piano keyboard with

my actual fingers. These academics had their heads so far up
Sonata Form they'd forgotten how to really listen; I'd remind
them.

It was a devil of a piece, so I practised it every day in an
empty hall on one of the college's Steinway grands. I practised so much my fingers hurt: the impossible runs in the
third movement, the string of parallel fifths where my hands
tumbled over each other. Then there were the scales and
arpeggios and Hanon finger exercises. I did those first thing
in the morning, picturing my new neighbour, the body
builder, putting a pillow over his head. There was also the
small question of committing this piece to memory. I'd be
playing without sheet music on the night. The trick was to
start randomly, at any given point, and see if I could continue. I was starting to really knock it into shape, this Ravel.
It was sounding polished.

I discovered another piece around this time which I
practised alongside the concerto. It was a piano sonata by
a Czech composer named Gideon Klein. He'd written it in
Theresienstadt concentration camp, where my own family
members had been; he later died in Auschwitz aged twenty-
six. I was mesmerized by it. The harmony seemed at first
atonal, but it wasn't absent of melody; a line strained upwards,
reaching out for something unattainable, the way my mother's
sculptures did. I played it over and over, not really perfecting
it, more meditating on Grandpa's brother, thinking about his
sacrifice. I also thought about my grandfather's turmoil at not
being able to convince his parents to leave Těšín, at leaving
them behind to get murdered. I got lost in sound. I launched
my fingers up and down the keyboard and wrestled with

the wrathful, crunching chords. Sometimes I felt like I was steering a speeding car, out of control. Other times my brain lagged, and I had strange moments of disconnection, as if my fingers were Gideon Klein's and not mine, as if someone else was doing the playing.

I finished up practising late each evening and crossed the college green. I stared up at the wide Cambridge skyline – the cloud formations, the dappling of light, the darkening heavens – and thought of my grandfather's parents being rounded up in Český Těšín and marched away into the night.

§

It was dead people's autographs I was after these days. I sold my duplicates of the living to pen pals and bought dead ones at auction with the proceeds. I also managed to get a few signed items from the antiquarian booksellers in Cambridge town centre: a numbered Edmund Blunden book of poetry and an old autograph book that had Churchill in it. I stared at the handwriting, passed my fingers across the grooves left by the fountain pen and felt something I couldn't explain: that a dead person had once been alive; that here was the proof.

My first ever autograph catalogue was prepared from my college bedroom: fifty items with brief descriptions – mostly signed album pages by Hollywood greats. The Blunden book went in. The Churchill signature was the star item. I stapled the pages together with some photocopies at the back, and posted them to pen pals, and to the new *Inkwell* collectors listed in the back of the past six months' issues. It was mail order only, and I provided my college address. People could send cheques and list their first, second and third choices, in case items were sold.

Despite my dwindling interest in living celebrities, when it was mentioned that Salman Rushdie would be putting in a rare appearance at Waterstones, I was willing to make a concession. Rushdie was a marked man, after all. Five years had passed since he'd unleashed something terrible. From one day to the next, he'd been whisked from his old life into a new and frightening existence: millions of people baying for his blood, demanding retribution. With a police escort at all times, he had to know about the book burnings and the real threats to his life. It crossed my mind that a signed copy of *The Satanic Verses* might be worth some real money, especially if someone managed to take Rushdie out. I paid for a ticket to the event, which was announced a few hours beforehand, and bought a copy of the book in preparation. Only a week to go till my Ravel performance, but I took the night off from practising. I knew every nook and cranny of that piece. I could practically play it backwards.

Waterstones was turned into a mini airport for the occasion. There were special scanners you had to walk through, and bags were put through a machine or manually searched. Police officers guided everyone inside. Carrie was with me because she was a fan of Rushdie's. I'd never read a word of his writing, myself; I just wanted to get the man to sign. The event was held upstairs. We took our seats. Hushed anticipation passed over the crowd. I felt we'd penetrated an inner circle – the mysterious locus where the condemned resided. I imagined the complex negotiations that had to have taken place: the phone calls, the protocols, the swearing to secrecy. And, then, in he strolled. He had a bounce in his step and a pot belly and seemed keen to get going. He looked surprisingly healthy, I thought. What Rushdie really wanted to do, it turned out, was read to us from his latest book.

He read well; I had to hand it to him. He did special voices for the different characters, just the way my dad might have, and performed it all like a little play written by someone else. He was clearly enjoying his moment. Honestly, I'd rather have heard about the fatwa, or the night he got taken away by special forces, or how he managed to get out of bed in the morning when entire countries wanted him dead. But the guy wanted to feel normal for a night. He wanted to do a regular book reading. I wondered how he was able to put all of that to the back of his mind, how he was able to put on such a good show.

At the end, he sat at a desk and you could queue up to get books signed. I was clutching my *Satanic Verses*, uncertain whether he'd cooperate. I expected his eyes to rise slowly as if facing his assassin, as if expecting the click of a timer. But when I handed him the book, he simply threw it open and signed his name across the title page. Unflinchingly. I watched his hand curving up and down as he completed his signature. Then he gave me a perfunctory smile. And that was it.

'I thought he'd seem a bit more – I don't know – *worried*?' I said to Carrie, as we made our way out through the Waterstones back entrance, which was manned by a cheerful police officer.

'Did you want him to be worried?' asked Carrie.

'A bit, I suppose. Twitchy, at least. Half the world wants him dead. He acted like he doesn't have a care in the world. Weird.'

'I think he has a few cares, Adam. He's staring death in the face every day. Frankly, he's brave to have shown up. You, my friend, are the weird one.'

'Maybe. But don't you think it's odd he signed *Satanic Verses*? Didn't even hesitate?'

We walked back to college, me clutching my signed book like a hunting trophy.

'So, come on then, how much is it worth?' asked Carrie.

'I don't know. Two hundred quid? Three hundred? I've never seen one.'

When we got to my room, we smoked weed and put Nas on the stereo:

> *Life's a bitch and then you die*
> *That's why we get high*

We decided another Ouija board was in order.

'How did you die?' we asked a churlish spirit.

'M-U-R-D-E-R,' the wine glass spelt out in nasty, jerky movements.

Carrie and I exchanged excited looks of terror.

'Jesus,' she said.

'How exactly were you murdered?' I asked.

The wine glass painstakingly jabbed at the letters one by one.

'H-I-T-L-E-R.'

'Oh my God,' said Carrie. 'Did it really just say Hitler?'

Then it spelt out 'G-I-D-E-O-N'.

'Is that your name?' I shouted.

'YES.'

'Shit, are you Gideon Klein?'

'YES.'

'Isn't that your Holocaust composer?' asked Carrie.

'YES,' said the wine glass.

I felt a chill go through my body when the glass spelt out its next message.

'E-N-J-O-Y L-I-F-E W-H-I-L-E I-T L-A-S-T-S.'

Then it stopped still.

§

My whole family turned up for the piano concerto. I scrubbed my face thoroughly with soap before greeting them, worried they'd smell the stench of cigarettes, the collision of their world into mine unsettling. When I got to the chapel, Grandpa Jožka and Grandma Lotka were fully taking in their ornate surroundings. My grandfather was likely thinking about his humble beginnings in Czechoslovakia, marvelling at the idea that a grandson of his could have anything to do with a place like this.

'My favourite grandson,' he said, 'good luck!' He flashed his winning smile and showed me the whites of his eyes, as if he and I were sealing one of his business deals together.

My sister, Ruth, had made the trip from Durham for the occasion. She ran over, squeezed me and told me how proud she was. My parents hovered on either side of her. My poor mother had her anxious look. I couldn't be sure if it was nerves about my performance or another drama unfolding with Dad – or with Grandma Lily, who'd been manhandled into an aisle seat.

'I hope it goes well, Doobs,' said my father, stroking my cheek. 'A son of mine performing a concerto in King's College Chapel! Who'd have thunk it? When I remember the house where I grew up in Tottenham. We had an outside toilet, you know – I must have told you how we were evicted. And now, this! My son, the success.'

He spread his arms out as if the chapel had been erected in his honour. I noticed how shiny he looked in his suit, with his freshly brushed curls. He bounced on his heels – so pleased to be here, so content within his own skin – and a part of me wanted to kill him.

The orchestra started up, and I played the opening cascade of notes. The flute had the tune. In the corner of my eye I could see five hundred audience members. I spotted where the Provost of the college was sitting with friends, one leg crossed over the other. My director of studies was nearby, my analysis tutor on the opposite side of the aisle. And I knew exactly where my family were sitting in a tight clump. I thought of the sad look on Mum's face, and her sculptures, and the Gideon Klein piece. I can't save her, I thought, which was exactly what my counsellor kept saying — a concise, serious woman I saw once a week at her house near Midsummer Common. It wasn't my job, and I couldn't do it. I thought of my grandfather's joy at being here, at the consolations he continually found in life. I wanted to be part of that consolation. Then I pictured my father, bristling with pride, his lip quivering at the idea that all this could have sprung from his loins. And something twisted in my stomach.

'We're going to die,' Carrie had said to me at lunchtime, apropos of nothing.

That line played again in my head.

'We are,' I'd said. 'Josh will die. Paul will die. Look.' I pointed to our friends sloping down King's Parade. 'That's a street full of dead people out there.'

'It's horrific,' Carrie sniggered. 'All so fucking pointless.'

I had to concentrate. I was playing without sheet music. I glanced up at the conductor, who was nodding furiously, his arms flailing about.

This is me playing my concerto, I thought. It's the moment of it happening. We reached the bit where the orchestra stopped, and it was just me – the spooky little Spanish tune, then the lyrical section with the splashes of bitonal colour. Then we got to the fast bit. I'd practised it a hundred times: the rhythmic punchy section with the Gershwinian ripples down, followed by the percussive segment. I caught my father's peeping eyes in the audience. I thought of the handwritten letter in his combination briefcase. He gets away with everything, I ruminated. Then I stared at my hands. They were flying up and down the keyboard. Who was making them do that? The same thing as happened with that Klein piece – another force taking over. For a full two or three seconds the hands were moving, playing the piece all by themselves. I wasn't doing anything except observing. It was an astonishing sight.

And then it fell horribly apart. My hands were hurtling across the keyboard hitting bum notes, like Les Dawson. I had no idea where we were in the piece. I'd completely lost my place. Five hundred people in the audience. I tried to refind where I was in the music. I'd practised it so many times – starting somewhere and carrying on. But it was no good. I couldn't find the notes. I held my hand up to the conductor. He looked baffled. His arms were still waving, the orchestra still going.

'We have to stop!' I yelled. 'We have to start again!'

And, my God, start again we did. The conductor brought the orchestra to a halt, and we went from the top. My hands started the opening cascades. Fuck, fuck, fuck, fuck, fuck. Was this really happening? Everyone's worst nightmare, and I was living it out. Start again? Who did that? And why was I even doing this concert? Then, as I played on, a further concern rose in me to a crescendo: I had to somehow think ahead to the place where it had fallen apart – I had to play the right notes while trying to remember what was supposed to happen next, up ahead. I didn't know. I didn't know.

The whole audience had watched me going wrong. My tutors had seen it. They were likely worried I'd fail again. The only thing to do, the only possible thing, was to somehow trust that my hands knew what they were doing. I'd practised till kingdom come. I knew this piece. As we got closer to the bit where I'd gone wrong, I made myself let go mentally, tried to stop controlling things. I'd watched my fingers play this piece before. I again thought of the practice I'd done – with the metronome, without it, at tempo, and as slowly and deliberately as I could without losing the will to live.

I had a thought as I watched my hands and willed them to play the right notes: if it happened again, if I went wrong, I would run out of the chapel. Yes, that was the plan! I'd sprint out past my parents and the Provost, past my tutors and my grandparents, and I'd keep on running. They'd look for me afterwards, but they'd never find me. I'd have run to

Grantchester or beyond. A picture came to mind of Rushdie heading to one of his safe houses; a night-time manoeuvre in the back of a van. Someone handing him a hot cocoa, and him staring out at the darkening sky.

HARRY SECOMBE

Harry Secombe (signature)

Then I hit on a plan.
To try to draw her attention
I set fire to myself. It moved her.
She fried an egg on me.

Harry Secombe
as Neddie Toulouse-Lautrec
in *The Goon Show*

My time at Cambridge fizzled out with the death of Grandma Lotka. In the middle of my third year at college, the doctors opened her up at Northwick Park Hospital and found inoperable cancer in her bowels. She was given three months to live. I drove to and from London in my Nissan Laurel to sit by her side, to hold her hand – a cigarette and a pack of mints on the way out, ten cigarettes on the way back. She was brave, never complained, made plans for a future we knew would never transpire. Opening her eyes after a deep sleep, she once declared, 'The Canaries – I'd like to go to the Canaries next summer. We can all go!'

Then she stopped eating.

'But she has to eat!' Grandpa Jožka barked at my mother. 'How can one continue without food? And this lying in bed is no good, either. She must fight it. She must get up!'

'But, Daddy, don't you understand? She can't eat,' explained my exasperated mother. 'She feels nauseous. And she doesn't have the energy to get up. She has cancer.'

My grandfather opened his hands in bafflement. It didn't make sense. After several minutes of sighing and knitting his brow, as if forced to witness a business deal going horribly wrong, he took his leave – pecked my grandmother on the cheek and wagged his finger.

'Now, *zlato*. Please – *try* to eat something.'

The door clicked shut behind him, and my grandmother said, 'Next time you speak to him, do me a favour. Tell him I roller-skated to Pinner and ate a pizza.'

I raced back to Cambridge at 100 mph, then continued the drive in the college bar on a Grand Prix video game, coast to coast across North America. When friends began to flock, we relocated to the quiz machine, where we shouted out the answers. I amused with my knowledge of long-forgotten Doris Day films and Tony Curtis's real name: Bernard Schwartz. Pretty soon, the beeping machines, the three-month time limit, the soft feel of my grandmother's hand, receded into the distance. I was back at college with a fugue to write and joints to roll.

As the weeks ticked by my grandmother lost more and more weight. The cancer really revealed her. As she approached death, she never looked better. She slept a lot more now, and when she woke was often too weak to talk. On one occasion she had a faraway look in her eye, and my mother said, 'Are you thinking about people from the past?' and by that it was obvious she meant the schoolfriends and aunties and uncles and cousins who'd vanished by the time my grandparents returned to Czechoslovakia in 1946. Grandma Lotka turned her head to catch my mother's eye and nodded gravely.

She was cremated in Hoop Lane. They played Smetana's *Má Vlast*, evoking the lolloping journey of the great Bohemian river, the Vltava. With her coffin up there on the stage, I felt she was canonized. In death, my grandmother had achieved a new and awesome status. It made me spool through my memories afresh, re-examining and reassessing the person my grandmother had been with a collector's fastidiousness. It made sense now that when a celebrity died, their autograph went up in value: Miles Davis's doubled, Audrey Hepburn's quadrupled.

My grandfather cut a strange figure at the funeral. He didn't cry, but then that wasn't his style. He'd never once shed a tear about what happened to his own parents, according to Mum. And now he stood with his hands behind his back, with a careful look of formality, as if grief was a humiliating inconvenience, as if to convey that he understood this role of widower, knew exactly how to play it. Of course, he couldn't have known; he couldn't have had the first idea.

A colourful gaggle of my grandparents' friends attended, all shaking their heads at the untimely demise – seventy-one, no age – and I felt my grandmother had been the glue that stuck a lot of people together. A woman called Mrs Rotte attended alone. She took a bus all the way from Bayswater. She was the one who made all the *vanilkové rohlíčky* and put them in shoeboxes, dusted them in icing sugar, separated them with thin paper. I knew my grandmother mostly ordered biscuits from Mrs Rotte because she felt sorry for her; she'd had a hard life and was a big talker. Now this woman stood in front of me and carefully searched for the right words to say.

'She was a nice woman,' she said, eventually, in a thick Czech accent.

And that was the most moving thing anyone said to me that day.

§

My grandmother's death lent a frantic quality to my remaining few months at college. With my family now beckoning from London, silhouetted ominously against the skies, I felt determined to make the most of what freedom was still available. So, it made total sense to get caught up in three simultaneous flings with female friends. I couldn't choose was the problem; I wanted to share myself freely; I loved them all with the vehemence of a man who'd tasted death and wanted to live. They all ended up pretty pissed off, and I ended up with none of them.

I hosted the usual séances with aplomb. I chuffed my way through the Marlboro Lights. I stalked the college bar late at night in search of company, just at the very moment when company became the rarest of commodities; everyone was revising, except me. My university days felt cut short, unexpectedly withdrawn – like Grandma Lotka. I'd been sure, for three years, that I'd been flowing down a tributary stream heading towards some great river, only to now discover a severe shoreline up ahead.

My finals were a joke. Beyond a joke. I borrowed three essays on acoustics from friends and learnt them by heart. I had no idea what they meant, any of them; I simply wrote them out in the exam room. The challenge was to match each essay up to the right question. Then I was obliged to compose a fugue under exam conditions without access to a piano. They gave you a tune, and you had two hours to invent a four-part fugue out of it, a torture so heinous it was surely somewhere in the small print of the Geneva Convention. My composition would have caused even Arnold Schoenberg to turn in his grave, and he was the guy who came up with the twelve-tone technique – essentially, music that sounded bad intentionally. Rachel came to Cambridge to help me revise. She drove down in her red Mini, ran out of petrol en route, and had to pawn her coat at the petrol station. We became lovers again; she made me stay up all night learning about nineteenth-century Italian opera.

'No, no, no – you mean *Bellini*!' corrected Rachel. 'The one with the long melodies and uncanny ability to match music with text.'

'I thought that was a drink.'

On results day, I wandered over to the Senate House then back to my room again, inglorious. I'd achieved what was commonly known as a "Desmond". A 2:2. I lit a cigarette and put on Prince's 'The Most Beautiful Girl in the World'. I took in the view of King's Parade – my view – and thought of Rachel, also my grandmother. And, with that, my business at Cambridge University was concluded. Now that my Nissan Laurel had come to its own untimely end – exponential self-acceleration over 60mph leading to total engine collapse – my dad had to pick me up in the Volvo. We eased our way out of the town centre, and my three years of partying, not working, quiz-machining, laughing, smoking, drinking, séancing, dancing – dancing! – came to an abrupt end.

'Now, have I told you the joke about the Jewish house-wife?' asked my father as we careered towards the M11 in the Volvo. 'She asks her husband, "So, darling, do you notice anything different about me?"'

'I know this one, Dad.'

'"You're wearing a new dress?" the husband says. "No," she says. "You've had your nails done?"'

'I know the joke,' I interrupted. 'You've told me a hundred times. She's wearing a gas mask.'

'Ah, that's right. You know it,' said Dad, tapping the steering wheel. 'Ah, well.'

§

Being back home in Pinner wasn't easy. My parents danced around each other much as before, but more remotely, as if my father had become one of those planets they discover orbiting the sun from an impossibly vast distance away. Adrian's orbiting was done in the form of Israeli folk dancing. He did all-night dance "marathons" now, two weekly classes, and the two summer camps he enrolled in required all-year-round preparation. The photo albums documenting these activities were never out of reach.

'I'm grieving, Adrian,' Mum said, pushing away a blurred picture of her husband sitting on Yitzchak Golan's shoulders, wearing a Hassidic beard. 'Do you think I want to see that?'

'Well, I don't know,' said Adrian, wearing his offended smile. 'It's good to be distracted sometimes.'

'I don't want a distraction. I want to grieve. My mother's been dead for four months.'

§

My parents' crumbling marriage notwithstanding, the main problem now was how to keep my twenty-a-day smoking habit a secret. If my mother found out, she'd make speeches about cancer, how she'd already lost a mother to that, then she'd lie awake at night worrying. I tried giving up, but it was hopeless. I wrote phrases on scraps of paper and stuffed them into my pockets – when I wanted a cigarette, I reached for those instead. 'I'm sorry to say you have stage four cancer' or 'Unfortunately there's a tumour the size of an aubergine in your left lung.' They didn't work. They only made me want a cigarette to process the bad news.

It turned out that as much as I loved my mother, I loved nicotine more. But how to disguise such a chronic habit? My tactic was simple. I invented arrangements with friends that began earlier and earlier in the day, finding I could just about get to 2 p.m. without looking like a dysentery sufferer waiting outside a locked public convenience. Then I'd go to the pub and smoke five cigarettes back to back, inhaling like the devil, as if my soon-to-be-cut-short life depended on it. While I waited for evening to arrive, I had a go on the fruit machines. I usually had three or four hours to kill until a legitimate arrangement came into view. I spent money. I lost money. I raided the bank account I'd set up after my bar mitzvah and started spending that. I didn't know why. I watched the cherries flashing and wondered what was supposed to happen next. I had no plans, no direction. I couldn't taste freedom any more. I stayed out each night till midnight and beyond, past my mother's bedtime.

Sometimes I saw Rachel, but mostly not. Her parents had money worries now. The clothes shop they ran together had gone into liquidation. They were selling their house, making plans to move to the coast. A dear university friend of Rachel's had taken his own life. It sent Rachel into spirals of unhappiness, and she wanted to get away – to Edinburgh, to work in an art gallery. Her plans didn't seem to include me. So, it was pubs and cigarettes and fruit machines for now. Each night, I drove home and threw my tobacco-infused clothes in a heap on the floor and fell into a clawing sleep.

'Smoky pub,' I'd explain, next day, when my mother screwed up her face at the stench.

'You don't smoke, do you?'

'Course not.'

'Well, I'm glad you're enjoying yourself,' said my mother, 'but you do need to start thinking about getting a job.'

'A job?'

I wasn't aware I was looking for one of those. There'd been the idea of becoming a concert pianist, but that dream had faded. Ravel had put paid to it. I'd wondered once or twice about 'impresario' after organizing an Indian concert in King's College Chapel during my second year. That had been a kick – the bellowing of the sitar, the fruity echo of tabla rebounding off Henry VIII's stained-glass windows – but now I was back in Pinner, it didn't appeal. Trouble was, there was nothing I really wanted to *do*.

'I've got an idea,' said Adrian. 'I'll speak to a client of mine. She organizes concerts – very successful. She might know someone who can help.'

I eyed my father as if he was some immovable object in my line of sight.

'Yes, OK,' I said. 'Ask.'

§

My father's client suggested a meeting with a man named Richard Korda, a music manager with an office on the Holloway Road. Apparently, he was looking for someone in relation to an upcoming extravaganza at the Albert Hall – a tribute to Ira Gershwin. His office was above a grocery shop. It took me some time to find the right buzzer to press. Once inside, a dusty staircase led to a small office covered with framed flyers and posters from West End shows. The original *Cats* poster was featured, and *Aspects of Love*. Korda was a wide man who wore braces and only ever smoked the first half of a cigarette. The second half got thrown away or was left smoking in an ashtray, as if on the instructions of some quack doctor.

'Adam!' he boomed, as if he and I were old friends.

His grin was almost as wide as his waist; I later learnt Korda had been a used-car salesman.

'Now, what instrument do you play?'

'Well, piano mostly, I said. 'I was planning to be a classical pianist originally, but then I had this awful experience playing a concerto in King's Chapel where I forgot the music halfway. Everyone's worst nightmare. I had to start again. Thank God it went fine the second time, but I'm not sure I'd ever . . .'

Korda looked confused. 'So, keyboard, then?' he asked.

'Yes. I could play a keyboard, I guess. Sure.'

I brought to mind the electric Casio Dad had installed in blind Grandma Lily's flat so she could entertain herself. Her rendition of 'Danny Boy' was legendary, sounding like background music to a Hammer Horror. I felt a squelch of humiliation.

'And you're up for some dogsbody work?'

Korda leant back in his chair and put his feet up on the desk. Some papers fluttered; a small pile of booklets fell to the floor.

'Gotta start at the bottom and work your way up in this business, you know. We all did.'

'Sure,' I said. 'I'm up for it.'

'Excellent. You'll need a mobile phone, though. Do you have one?'

'Er, no.'

'Get one, will you, Adam? I'll be in touch.'

What followed was a race around London in my mum's Honda, akin to the plot of *Herbie Goes to Monte Carlo*. I was

a runner, earning £75 per day. I was breathless. I was effi-
cient. I was confused by my new career.

'Pick up some music from Stanmore, will you,' Korda
would yell down my mobile phone. 'And then – you're gonna
hate me – drive it to Balham, will you?'

'Balham?' I pulled over to consult the *A–Z*. 'Sure. That's
fine.'

A door opened in Stanmore. Music books were bundled
into my chest. Another door opened in Balham. I bundled
same into another man's chest. A break at a pub in Seven
Sisters – eighty quid down on the fruit machine – and my
mobile phone started twitching again.

'You couldn't pick me up in Angel and take me to the
Savoy, could you? Need to pick up Lorna Luft.'

'Sure.'

And there she was – Judy Garland's daughter – in the
back seat of the car, discussing the signature key for 'The
Man That Got Away'.

'F is too high, Richard. I'm not a soprano.'

'So, what key would you like, then, Lorna,' shouted
Korda, puffing on his cigarette, squished beside her in the
back. 'You say. You tell me. G? Do you want G? Or how
about B?'

'I think D would be fine,' said Luft, glancing out of the
window at the traffic.

'Well, then. D it is!' boomed Korda, slapping his thigh as
if D was a town we could all now drive to for a slap-up dinner.

§

The Ira Gershwin extravaganza came and went, and my
phone stopped ringing. So, what next? Korda had another

job for me: a Christmas show at the Oxford Playhouse, starring Harry Secombe. A keyboard player was needed for an evening performance – £100. I remembered Secombe from a radio show in the 1950s called *The Goon Show*. My father would put it on in the Volvo; a group of men squeaking and shouting and corpsing at their own jokes. I'd also seen the Secombe of later years on the TV programme *Highway*, performing high-pitched operatic versions of hymns to crowds of shepherds. Ugh. Yeah, I supposed I could do it.

The idea was to drive up for the matinee. Sit through that next to the keyboard player, so that I roughly knew the drill, then perform the evening show. It didn't quite work out that way. First, I went to a pub in Pinner and lost £150 on the fruit machine, my gambling fast developing into a habit more gruesome than my smoking. Then I drove to Oxford. Only, there were roadworks on the M40, so it took me three hours. And by the time I arrived, the afternoon performance had well and truly ended. The musicians were filing out to the green room. I had all of fifteen minutes to look through the music.

The show began, and I lost my place immediately – in the first bar. The tempo was really fast. I carried on playing, regardless, romping through, sight-reading – sight-reading, for Christ's sake! – slamming my hands on the keyboard the way I'd just slammed them on the fruit machines. Harry Secombe was on stage, cheering his fans with his old, stale routine. A nightmare, I thought; this is a nightmare! I tried to keep my eyes on the music. It wasn't that it was difficult, just that I'd never seen it before. Dotted around the page were markings where the keyboard was meant to change sound – '#44' or '#131' – but I ignored all those; just tried to somehow keep going. And then, gradually, I noticed that all the musicians around me were stopping playing, thinning out. What was going on? I still had music on my page. And then, suddenly, I was the only one playing – the only one! I was playing, and Secombe was singing. We were performing our very own pas de deux. My playing was shaky, but I was just about managing it. A note on the music demanded sleigh bells, but there was little chance of that. I saw Secombe notice the lack of cue. I saw the sweat on his brow as he lowered his eyes to look into the band pit. Who the hell was on keyboard? Not the usual guy.

I lingered backstage after the show. The conductor grimaced. He had a red beard and a flap of hair thrown over a balding head. He looked disgusted. He later phoned Korda to complain. And Secombe? In the old days, I'd have waited for an autograph. Part of me was still tempted. But then I heard someone asking after him.

'Oh, he's not feeling too well,' explained the conductor, taking a moment to stare me out. 'He's resting in his dressing room.'

'Not a single sodding sleigh bell!' I imagined Secombe squeaking at his manager, eyes watering as he threw back another paracetamol.

I returned to Pinner, humiliated, to find my mother home alone. Dad was out Israeli dancing. I ran upstairs to brush my teeth and shower, scrub the tobacco off my skin, make myself the right kind of son again. Then I told her what had happened. She laughed; for the first time since Grandma Lotka, she really laughed. 'Oh, that's terrible,' she said, but I could tell how she enjoyed the irreverence of it. A stagnant old comedian like Secombe and the new keyboard player stuck in a traffic jam, then sight-reading. 'That's funny,' she said, 'really funny. I've never liked Harry Secombe. His jokes are terrible.'

I smoked out of my window. I planned to duck back inside when my father's Volvo returned. But it didn't. The usual time of 11 p.m. came and went with no sign of him. Gone midnight, and he still wasn't back. Finally, his car appeared at 12.30 and sloped into the drive. I lay in bed listening to my parents' conversation. Adrian explained he'd run out of petrol – completely run out – never happened before. He'd had to walk a mile to fill a plastic can at a petrol station, he explained. I shook my head into my pillow.

Next morning, Billie Holiday was on my clock radio again, her voice filled with her same old heartfelt devotion to misfortune:

> *Good morning heartache,*
> *thought we said goodbye last night.*

JAWS

Once a Bond fan, always a Bond fan.

Richard Kiel

I pulled into the car park of the Landquist Hotel, a short mile away from Heathrow. My head was shaved like a convict's, Notorious B.I.G. blared through the speakers, and plastic bags filled with autographs careened across the back seats. I drove Grandma Lotka's low-slung Honda Civic these days and boy did it tear up the road. This was the car she sped to Brent Cross in, to get away from her husband's black moods. Nought to sixty in eight seconds. *Catch me,* zlato, *if you can!*

I traipsed my Sainsbury's bags inside the shiny, overly large reception area, whose industrial wood-panelling and fake chandeliers offered shine and celebration. The people checking out yawned, tapped the front desk, or sat beside piled-up luggage at the huge sliding entrance door. Unless I was very much mistaken, that was Patrick Moore, the astronomer, up ahead of me in the queue. And the chiselled guy with the fake tan, arguing with the receptionist about a ventilator shaft – that had to be George Lazenby, the actor who played Bond in the one Bond movie I'd never seen.

§

Showbiz was over for me. No more men with wide grins, no more dogsbody work, no more sleigh bells. I'd called it a day with the fruit machines, too, and their flashing lies. I was done with losing. I'd thrown my lot in with autographs as a career, at least for the time being, while I worked out what I really wanted to do. It was an easy way to make money –

I had a gaggle of collectors who sent me their want lists – and it prevented me from having to work for someone else. I was a dealer now, on the make, looking for pricing errors, taking opportunities.

One such opportunity came up at Bonhams. A lifetime collection of autographs, from the 1930s to the 1980s, offered in a single lot – everything from Charlie Chaplin to Harrison Ford, inscribed to a collector named Lionel. This collector had apparently spent his entire life waiting outside hotels and stage doors. My grandfather offered to lend me the necessary £10,000 to buy it, to help establish my business.

'But you have to pay me back,' he warned, eyeing me carefully across his kitchen table, jabbing a forbidding finger.

'Of course, Grandpa. As quickly as I can.'

'That's right. It's no good to owe money. Ach, you know who you remind me of? Myself, when I was a young man. I was an entrepreneur just like you! I started by changing money across the border. Later I got involved with some gold bars, but that turned into a nightmare. I had to run away for a while, which is a long story. But what I don't understand is how people pay money for these signatures. It's not artwork. There's no skill involved. Just a signature on a piece of paper. Unbelievable.'

The kitchen clock ticked. Everything in the house was dead still.

'It's so quiet here,' complained my grandfather.

He shook his head and looked deep into my soul, as if I might be able to do something about his situation, might have the right authority. I imagined him staring into the eyes of bank managers the same way, years earlier, when he started up his firm in London after the war and needed a loan of his own.

All I could think to say was, 'I know, Grandpa. But you're doing so well.'

'You think so?' He laughed scornfully and slumped back in his chair. Then he leant forward again, hands clasped together. 'It's the quiet I can't get used to. And the loneliness.'

My mother was uneasy at first about the loan.

'My father's very complicated,' she said. 'He has a terrible temper. When I was a child, there were times he got so angry his face would go bright red and he'd stand at the sink gasping for breath. I used to worry he'd have a heart attack. And he talks about hitting me when I was a tiny child, because I wanted to get into my parents' bed. He says he smacked me until I fell asleep to teach me a lesson. Can you imagine? I was two years old. I can't bear to think about it. There was also that time, much later, that he threw a box of crockery at your father in the middle of an argument. I'm just saying, he's not someone you want to cross.'

'Well, I'm not going to do that, am I, Mum? Grandpa just wants to help me. I'll pay him back really quickly.'

'Be careful,' said my mother, anxiety settling around her lips.

I bought the collection, took apart the dozens of autograph albums and put all the individual signatures into display folders, all priced individually. I quickly made back several thousand pounds from dealers on the Strand and Cecil Court, off Charing Cross Road, where the second-hand book shops were. I managed to pay back a chunk of the loan.

'But don't you want to *keep* some of these?' asked Adrian, flicking restlessly through my albums, pausing at the Marx Brothers to offer his Stan Laurel sad face.

I had little time for his sappiness. 'Can't afford to,' I said. 'I'm a dealer now.'

'Seems a shame, Doobs. Some of these are such nice examples.'

I set up a basic website – a list of items without illustrations – and got myself my very first email address. I took out a regular advert in *The Inkwell* and sat on eBay all day long waiting for the phone to ring. The fax machine was a discovery. I could photocopy autographs, then fax copies to collectors. Sometimes, in haste, I passed the actual autographs through the machine, crossing my fingers they wouldn't shred. Otherwise, I sat sifting through a rolling wave of auction listings. I sometimes waited whole minutes for the pages to load, the little images popping open like flowers, while the larger ones unravelled spasmodically, pixel by pixel, slow-turning into yet another fake signed photo of Leonardo DiCaprio.

I was operating my business from my old bedroom in Pinner, but I'd moved in with Rachel now. We were renting a simply furnished place in Harlesden. Part of an ill-conceived house conversion, the room layout was higgledy-piggledy, with an over-abundance of carpet and corridor and an extra bit of staircase leading nowhere. We smoked. We drank cheap wine. We hoovered. We made meals we remembered our mothers making. Then, when we'd had it with the spaghetti bolognese, we headed to Starburger on the edgy bit of the high road. Either that, or we'd get a takeaway from the

Chinese on the corner, where you waited with the angsty customers while the food got thrown around metal cauldrons. We spent our evenings with friends at pubs, gossiping about landlords and 'which of you does the washing up?' One of us would unfurl a ten-pound note to pay.

Now that we were playing at being adults, these banknotes took on a different meaning – no longer the Monopoly money of old. Landlords evicted people; courts fined them. No dollar, no burger. But we bore our new financial pressure with bonhomie. We were hard up, sure, but we styled it out, surfed sleekly on the Lake of Pennilessness, took breaks to sun ourselves on its shoreline. We were young. We were the thing. Rachel got a job as an art teacher at a primary school and started a part-time training course to become a psychotherapist, while I drove to my old bedroom in Pinner each morning and waited for the Americans to buy pieces of paper. We reconvened at night to laugh off our drudgery.

My advert quickly provided me with a handful of regular clients: a woman in New York, Roberta Hernandez, interested in actors and actresses who'd killed themselves or died young of drugs overdoses, or been famous for such a short time that only she had heard of them; I received regular frantic calls from phone booths in Manhattan asking me what was new.

'Well, let me think, I have a rare signature of Belinda Lee.'

'Belinda who?'

'British actress. She died at the age of thirty-five in a car crash. Inscribed to someone called Lionel.'

'I want that,' Roberta bleated. 'Put it to one side. Now, you don't have a Lottie Pickford, do you? Mary's younger sister? Heart attack at forty-three.'

Then there was Raymond Funamoto in Hawaii, who collected the autographs of *Carry On* actors.

'I'm really looking for a handwritten letter by Charles
Hawtrey,' he frequently explained, bravely riding the five-
second time delay.

There was a woman who lived in a lighthouse on Lake
Ontario, featuring 113 framed signed photographs of
Laurence Olivier; a woman in Michigan with verbal diar-
rhoea and an unquenchable appetite for Shirley Temple; a
Texan who continually phoned to ask, with great courteous-
ness, for 'unsuccessful presidential candidates'.

§

The autograph convention consisted of one large room for
the dealers' stalls and another adjoining one for the guest
celebrities. Each of the stars had a selection of unsigned 8×10
poses fanned out on their desks in front of them, showing
them in the prime of their lives, when they were the thing,
in their most famous roles, beside their best-known co-stars.
You could choose the pose you wanted, and they signed it
for you for a fee ranging from £10 to £25, depending on how
"big" they were. Patrick Moore was £10; George Lazenby,
£20. If you wanted a picture taken with the celebrity, a photographer was on hand. The photos were developed in-house
within two hours, and then you could get them signed.

The famous people sat slumped in chairs, po-faced, old,
mostly unrecognizable. I had to screw up my eyes for a full
five seconds before the middle-aged woman with the white
scarf and caved-in cheeks turned into my first ever crush:
Margot Kidder, the actress who played Lois Lane. If I closed
one eye, it made sense that the miniature actor clambering

onto the tartan-upholstered chair had once been an Ewok. But there was no mistaking enormous Richard Kiel, the actor who'd played Jaws in the Bond movies. The seven-foot-two actor strode carefully, unsmilingly – a golem – across the carpet. He was wearing a geometric haircut that brought out his – well, his teeth. I stared uneasily, remembering the way his face contorted when he bit into the cable car wire in *Moonraker.* I recalled the vitriolic anger Jaws could summon on demand, the look of glee whenever given the opportunity to kill.

I settled into my seat in the dealer room: fifty or so wooden tables splashed with autographs. The collectors strolled up and down the aisles, their eyelines fixed at desk level, also groin level, surveying the goods on offer.

'I've got a better Sean Connery than that,' was one collector's opener, waving his hand at my signed 8×10 still from *Medicine Man.* 'Mine's from *Goldfinger.* He's lying on the bed and the laser's going up his leg – signed in the light portion. Gert Fröbe's signed too – you know, the one who played Goldfinger. How much is that worth, then?' The collector looked at me for the first time, focusing his eyes somewhere behind my head.

'I don't know. Maybe three hundred pounds?'

'I'd have thought so. Paid a hundred.' The collector chuckled to himself, then continued flicking through my binder.

Here was my old pen pal Darren Pendle. I'd never met him before. He was thin and nervy, with a tight smile hitched a little high – like his trousers. He was a man of few words – grabbed hold of his chin in lieu of speaking – and we were pretty much done after 'hello'. 'Nice Hepburn,' he said, eventually.

Movie Guy turned up. He didn't bother with pleasantries, simply withdrew from his briefcase a signed 7×5 photo of Bela Lugosi as Dracula, lips parted, going in for the bite, signed in blood-red ink. He displayed it against his chest.

'Just picked this up, Adam. What do you think?'

'Looks authentic,' I said. 'Lugosi used to sign in red a lot in the 1950s, when he was on stage in London.'

'Excellent. Now, let's see what *you've* got.'

I glanced down at my autographs facing outwards. What I'd have given to own some of these a few years earlier. I remembered suddenly the small collection of cheques and banknotes folded up in my pocket, totalling £850 on the last count – our rent was £250 a week. I was pleased, but it also felt too easy, somehow – no skill involved. My grandfather's comments about autographs being artless returned to me. Plus, now that I wasn't a collector any more, I had the uncanny feeling I was profiting from a previous version of myself, essentially sucking my own blood; not a million miles from how Margot Kidder had to be feeling next door, signing that shot of her flying with Superman, eyes full of longing, hand outstretched.

The bar was alive that night. I sipped a pint of beer while a quartet of fellow dealers compared spoils from the day. There'd been a celebrity dinner – I hadn't been able to afford it – £75 per ticket – and various anecdotes now flowed about someone telling saucy jokes to Liz Fraser, someone getting a free autograph from a drunk Ewok, someone else having a fractious exchange with George Lazenby about the Bond films he'd turned down. Sig Bernstein joined now, adjudicating everything with a wry smile and shake of his head, in concert.

Rachel phoned me on the mobile, which gave me the opportunity to perform some circuits of the hotel lobby and tell her about the convention.

'Not sure quite how to describe this,' I said. 'To give you an idea, Lois Lane's having a drink at the bar with Darth Vader.'

'But you've sold a few things. That's good!' Rachel proffered.

I thought about calling my father to tell him about my success, but he'd only ask me what I'd sold and say, 'Oh, what a shame' and make crestfallen noises down the phone. So, I called my grandfather instead. He'd be suitably delighted.

He was. He chuckled at the other end.

'My grandson, the k'nacker,' he said. 'Just like I was at your age – a real businessman.'

'Thanks, Grandpa.'

'But one thing,' he said. His voice was suddenly stern. 'Don't spend it on wasteful things.'

'Not at all, Grandpa,' I said nervously, conscious of wanting to pacify; conscious also of the pint of beer in my other hand, and the box of Marlboro Lights in my pocket. I wondered, fleetingly, what my grandfather would do if he knew. Might his face contort and go red? What might he throw at my head?

'I'll give you a cheque as soon as the money's in my account,' I added, frantically. 'I want to pay you back.'

'Very good. *That's* the right answer, my grandson. It's never good to owe money.'

I woke early for the hotel buffet, which was included with the room. The other dealers and collectors were already there. Movie Guy was sipping a glass of champagne and negotiating an A4 omelette. Darren Pendle was operating the toast machine. I piled my plate high with pre-scrambled eggs and congealed bacon and took my place among my brethren. Sig Bernstein threw down a plate of kippers beside me.

'Known him since he was a kid,' he barked at the others, smirking with pleasure. 'Came to postcard fairs with his father. Brought his collection to show me. Bunch of secretarials. It was sad.'

'Well, that was when I first started collecting,' I tried, facing down the trio of glistening faces. 'I didn't know about secretarials then. I was just a kid.'

'You're still a kid,' laughed Bernstein, nastily. 'You name it, he had it.'

Kill me now, I thought.

'Worst Neil Armstrong Autopen I ever saw,' continued Bernstein. 'Clint Eastwood to make your eyes water, Laurence Olivier signed by his daughter, printed Sinatra. I felt bad telling him.'

The others widened their eyes and goaded Bernstein on with little giggles and side-smiles. These people aren't dealers, I thought; they're collectors, like Adrian. I sure as hell wasn't one of them. I was here for the money, nothing else. Then, something caught my attention in the corner. Richard Kiel, the seven-foot monster, sitting all alone, peacefully contemplating a small portion of what looked like twigs – some kind of muesli.

'Jesus, look at Jaws,' said Darren Pendle, becoming lively. 'That's exactly how he looked in *The Spy Who Loved Me* when Barbara Bach pulled the gun on him – remember? If looks could kill! Has Patrick Moore upset him again?' He let out a feeble laugh, and the others joined in.

'Maybe that's just his face,' intoned Movie Guy, shaking with laughter.

I had half an eye on the enormous ex-actor for the rest of the day, far more interested in what was going on in his room than mine. By late morning, he'd been relegated to a giant wheelchair – crumbling spine, by all accounts – which made my heart sink. I wondered what it had been like for him, all these years, trudging around autograph conventions, the same hush of excitement at his real-life size every time he entered a room. I fancied this was on his mind, when at lunchtime I caught sight of him whizzing around the hotel reception area; whenever people dodged out of the way a subtle smile appeared on his lips.

Kiel was back fully installed at his table for the afternoon, looking resurrected and pale. I couldn't resist any longer. I approached his desk. A plastic VISA sign was taped to the curtain behind him.

'Hi,' I said.

The enormous man was chewing gum. He turned to fix his deadened eyes on me, perhaps fantasizing about the most satisfying way to kill me. Stick my head in the breakfast toaster machine?

He whined, 'The black-and-whites are fifteen. Twenty pounds gets you a choice of the colours.' He pointed towards a variety of violent images of himself from decades earlier.

But I wasn't after the Kiel of yesteryear. I was happy enough with present-day Kiel, warts and all.

'Could I get a photo with you, and have you sign it later?'

'Sure, we can do that,' said the actor, his face still dead-pan. 'That'll be twenty.'

I produced my wallet and noticed the giant's eyes linger on it. I withdrew my Visa and handed it to his assistant.

'I'll do the pose people like,' suggested Kiel. 'It's this.'

He reached his humungous hands around my head, one over the top, one under my chin – the brain-crushing pose. While Kiel's assistant operated the credit card machine – you could hear it whirring – Jaws and I manoeuvred our mouths into large and professional grins.

MARILYN

You're always running into
people's unconscious.

Marilyn Monroe
(née Norma Jeane Mortenson)

I answered my office phone to the sound of gargling.

'Catarrh,' explained a small voice. 'This is Ray from the postcard fair. Friend of your dad's. He wrote your number down on the thingy.'

I remembered him now from my teenage years: a short dealer with a white mullet who sct up in the same aisle as Sig Bernstein. He fished around inside cardboard boxes to retrieve his wares – old theatre programmes, posters, somebody's wartime schoolbooks – before spreading them out in a six-inch wedge across his stall. Then he stood beside the display scratching his head, as if wondering how on earth he'd got there.

'I've got an autograph book with Marilyn Monroe in. Thought you might be interested.'

Interested? Monroe was on every autograph collector's want list.

'But has she signed in red ink?'

I asked this in the manner of a medical specialist probing a patient for telltale symptoms. Because red ink always meant secretarial; red ink meant fake. You usually saw it on photos, the neat curly hand: 'love and kisses, Marilyn Monroe'. The real thing was another story: an intelligent, illegible scrawl, written at breakneck speed, the pen changing direction at least twice.

'Nah, don't think it's red. Hang on, I'll have a look. Soon tell you.'

Some fumbling. The sound of the receiver hitting the

floor. A woman shouting. A coughing fit, like a belt thrown around a tumble dryer.

'Here we go,' said Ray, taking back control. 'It's in black.'

'Right – well, that's good news. And how much were you hoping to sell it for?'

An almighty exhalation of air.

'Dunno,' said Ray. 'I was hoping you could tell me.'

'Hmm. Well, it's hard to say without seeing it,' I said, trying to maintain professional neutrality.

'Come see it, then. I'd have thought it's worth a couple hundred at least,' suggested Ray.

Not bad. Signatures were worth a thousand. I had access to an army of deranged Americans ready to hand over fistfuls of dollars for a page signed by Marilyn. Even Movie Guy would pay seven or eight hundred.

'Well, that sounds reasonable. Whereabouts are you, exactly? I might be able to drive over today.'

'Today? Come today. I'm not doing anything.'

'And you live where, Ray?'

'I'm in Penge.'

'Is that South London?' I clarified.

Ray wheezed a laugh at the other end. 'Could say that.'

I'd completed the Harlesden to Pinner leg first thing, and now it was Pinner to Penge, that little-known pilgrimage route.

The M25 was slow. People tapped steering wheels. The information board flashed out discouraging figures. Still, Marilyn's face beckoned: lips parted, eyes half-winking. I remembered the handful of times a really good signed photo had come up at auction – Christie's or Bonhams – the one in her negligee, mouth yawning open, or the Cecil Beaton photo she liked to sign in lacy white ink. The same Asian guy in the tight T-shirt always turned up to outbid me, or Bernstein pulled the plug from back in the doorway, or some American bid over the phone. Everyone was always grabbing her from my clutches.

What was it about Marilyn? Why did everyone want her? Not her acting, I didn't think. Nor her beauty. It had more to do with her shrewdness. I'd heard an interview once and sensed something uncannily astute motoring away beneath the surface, a grasp of her own complexities. Oh, and there was something else, something very appealing: you felt you couldn't hold on to Marilyn, no matter how hard you tried, because she was always disappearing elsewhere.

§

My father had moved out. Someone had told my mother about a woman at the Israeli dance class; how every Thursday night Adrian did couple dances with her, stared into her eyes. He gave her lifts back to Highgate, the source said. My mother promptly asked him to leave and sort his head out. They began couples counselling. My sister was still living in Durham, working with asylum seekers, offering them legal advice, so we communed over the phone. We were beside ourselves. The thing we'd both privately feared was finally transpiring, and now we had to watch it unfold from the sidelines.

My mother was permanently red-eyed. She'd lost her mother, and her children to university, and now this. But, really, it was just the latest downtick on the line graph plotting Adrian's descent into madness over the previous twenty years. The line's weaving journey took in his claustrophobic relationship with his mother, his workaholism, pathological need to dress up as a Hassid and fixation with the Holocaust. The case study was now retrospectively updated with Israeli dancing positioned as the gateway drug to infidelity.

'That was when he first started seeming quite crazy,' my mother reflected at the kitchen table in Pinner, tapping her cheek and describing an upward left–right curve with her eyes, like Hercule Poirot. 'Obsessional. All the skits he needed to perform, to be admired.'

'I don't know. I think it was before that,' I interpolated, linking my fingers and tapping my thumbs together. 'Remember in Paris, when Ruth and I were little, how he walked around the entire Picasso Museum without removing his video camera from his face?'

'Yes,' said my mother, shaking her head tiredly at the additional evidence. 'You're right. He did. But I never could have imagined him doing *this*.'

She couldn't? It hadn't been a surprise to me, exactly. But then, I hadn't told her about the letter from the woman in Amsterdam. I hadn't wanted to hurt her. I reached out to take my mother's hand. We sighed in unison.

'You know what I keep thinking about? It's silly, but I keep remembering that time Grandma Lotka left me at a residential summer camp. I can't have been more than eight or nine at the time. She drove me to a strange place in the countryside and left me there. Can you imagine? I was look-ing for my mummy everywhere, but she'd already left – driven back home. She must have thought she was doing the right thing. I don't know.'

A very faraway look now descended, and I felt my mother to be staring into the abyss again, the one that extended further and deeper than the length and breadth of Adrian, an abyss that extended into my childhood and beyond. I had that very old feeling of wanting to save her, wanting to whisk her away from what lay below. At twenty-two, I knew most of what was down there: the early misadventure with Adrian, the youthful naivety; then, lined up behind that, the domineering father contending with incalculable losses, the mother trying to survive; and, further back still, the horrifying losses themselves – the named and nameless relatives, the missing graves, the manner of death.

'Are you alright, Mum? You look upset.'

'I'm OK, darling. I'm fine. I think I'm just getting very tired of trying to understand everything.'

My father packed his bags and found a studio flat to rent opposite Regent's Park Mosque. It had a settee, a Formica table, a chair and a view directly onto the mosque entrance.

'Could be worse,' Adrian speculated, reclining on the black-leather settee with his hands behind his head. 'It's convenient for work. I can walk to the office. A bit far away from Grandma Lily, which is not ideal – ooh, that reminds me, I must give her a call in a few minutes. I do realize all this must be very strange for you, Doobs.'

'You could say that,' I said. 'Beyond strange. It's awful.'

'Look, Doobs, let's just hope Mummy and I can work things out in the counselling. That's the hope. There are plenty of things that still need to be said – not just by your mother, but by me too. You know, things I wouldn't want to say to you – she's your mother, of course I understand that – but I do need to say to her. For instance, I'm under such a lot of pressure from Grandma Lily, and your mother has never really taken away any of that from me.'

'She did organize those au pairs to live with her, didn't she?'

'Well, yes, that. But, you know, she could ring her from time to time. That would take a lot of strain off. And I understand – of course, I understand – she doesn't want to. My mother's not her type. She finds her very difficult.'

'I suppose she's not *her* mother, so . . .'

'I know, Doobs. I know. Oh, and by the way, *that's* not the reason for this. Not at all. It's just one of the things that's not been ideal for a while. And this person I met at the Israeli dancing, well, that was really just someone to talk to, to be honest, because I've been feeling very isolated for a long time. I've not been myself. And, don't worry, nothing's actually *happened* with this woman, if that's what you're worried about. I'm a married man. Of course, nothing untoward has taken place. But Mummy and I do need to work a few things out. We've neither of us been completely happy for a while. I need to give a bit of thought now to what I really want. Just a little bit. Look, let's see what happens.'

See what happens? Well, I didn't have much choice about that, did I? And think about what *he* wanted? When had he not done that? I heard in the inflection of my father's voice his own one-to-one counselling – some halfwit telling him he needed to find himself. The problem wasn't what my father needed or wanted, was my diagnosis; the problem was what my mother had never got. From him. Understanding!

He bought her presents, fussed and complimented her, he found her beautiful, he bolstered her confidence, but had he ever tried to understand her?

'Anyway,' said Adrian, 'I hope she's alright. I'm sure she's glad she's got you looking out for her. Gosh. I feel terrible about it all. It's not at all easy for me, any of this. I do still love her, you know. That's never stopped.'

My father blinked his eyes, then rested his head back on the settee. He held the pose for a second or two, then glanced at his watch and said, 'Shall we see if there's anything on TV?'

§

I was out every night with friends, and still asleep when Rachel left for work in the mornings. If I saw her it was for dinner, then I was off out.

'It's amazing how people play out their parents' patterns,' she said to me one evening, meaning the clients she was seeing as part of her psychotherapy training. 'Even when it's the one thing they're trying to avoid. It seems the compulsion to repeat is so strong.'

'I'd love to discuss it, but I'm going to be late,' I said, curtly, as if it was my behaviour she was hinting at.

'Well, have a nice time, then,' she said, rolling her eyes at my unfriendliness.

Was I being like my father, I wondered, as I disappeared off in the Honda? Was I being inattentive, neglectful, self-regarding, double-crossing, possibly mad? A surge of guilt passed through me as I considered the trajectory I was on. Was there anything I could do about it? Any way to stop it?

How ingrained was this behaviour? I thought back to King's College, where no one ever mentioned parents or patterns playing out. I only ever had the next six hours to contemplate back then. Now I had the rest of my life nagging away, stretching out in front of me like one of those long, empty freeways in Arizona.

We got stoned, me and my friend David. We laughed, we ate Chinese food, we talked about the important things, like duck in pancakes or our waiter's state of mind. Then we went to hear music – a modern-jazz gig at the Vortex, the room full of angry eyes, my feet trying to tap, except they couldn't because the music was in seven time, or was it eleven? Rachel came into my thoughts, and I wondered if she was asleep yet, wondered why I wasn't with her. After the concert, me and David talked in the car about God and death and consciousness.

'We're like marionettes,' I said, 'and life breathes through us. No, not marionettes – more like lamps – and the life flickers into us just like light, then it passes out again.'

I got back at 3 a.m., the earlier conversation with Rachel pulped to a blur. As I closed my eyes, the vague shape of it returned and I felt the need to kiss Rachel on the shoulder and tell her I loved her.

'What's wrong?' said Rachel, turning to check on me, a look of knowing in her eyes.

'Nothing.'

'Has anything happened? Are you OK?'

'I'm fine. Just wanted to tell you I love you.'

'I love you too. Go to sleep. Stop worrying.'

I shut my eyes and tried to find a dream to fall into. But

it was the one about my parents again: my mother alone in the double bed in Pinner and my father in the flat in Regent's Park. Alone? I wasn't sure. Eventually, I drifted into a dark sleep.

§

I decided to start my own therapy. I found an Australian psychotherapist who lived around the corner. He was cheerful and focused, likely good at barbecues. He had all the right books on depression and death and despair on his shelves, and was always good for a laugh. I enjoyed the idea of intimate conversation with a stranger, enjoyed presenting the various personalities of my family as if part of a grand puppet show – moving them around, positioning them on an imaginary stage. When we stopped talking about me, we could talk about me for a while. I wanted to make my therapist laugh. I wanted to be his favourite client.

Then we got down to the nitty-gritty. I was feeling stuck and depressed and guilty – guilty about what, I wasn't sure – and while I wanted to achieve great things in my life, I couldn't say much more about that either. I seemed to be having an issue with "becoming myself" and "feeling entitled", because those things seemed to entail leaving other people behind. Well, my mother, chiefly. And now that she'd been *actually* left behind by my father, I felt all the more responsible for her while knowing I couldn't really give her what she needed.

'So, you want to save her?' asked the Australian, looking me deep in the eyes.

'Well, I've always been the one she talks to,' I explained. 'I'm the one who knows her. And she needs me now more than ever, just when it's the moment for me to move on with my own life.'

'Are you sure?' asked the therapist. 'When you say you know her and know what she wants? You know her as a son, right? Not as a husband.'

'Well, yes. I see what you mean.'

I offered a laugh, but my therapist didn't laugh back; he knew he was on to something.

'And let's say you really could save her,' continued the Australian, 'which is definitely questionable. Is that really your responsibility?'

I thought for a moment, then conceded, 'I don't know. Maybe not.'

'And here's the bigger question.' The Australian cut the air with both hands, then leant right into me. 'Would you really want to?'

§

Ray was waiting in his doorway in Penge, wearing a white string vest, light-blue football shorts and an open pink dressing gown with fur trim.

'You made it,' he observed.

His home was ramshackle. There were piles of things everywhere – DVDs, underwear, PlayStation controls, handbags, hair accessories, newspapers – as if tipped out of one of those cardboard boxes he brought to the fairs.

'Awful traffic on the M25,' I said. 'Took me two hours.'

'Yeah, would do,' said Ray, nodding only slightly. 'So that's the book, then.' He inclined his head towards a cluttered dining table, and kept his hands firmly tucked in the pockets of his pink dressing gown.

A 1950s autograph album sat on the table beside an ornate antique tea set – the cups upside down on their saucers – and various dotted figurines of Chinese peasants.

I flicked past the usual messages from the schoolfriends of the owner. 'Roses are red, violets are blue, sugar is sweet and so are you – to dearest Jackie from Carole xxx'. Then past a couple of Adam Faiths, a Tommy Trinder, a Dickie Henderson, none of them worth a thing. I flicked and flicked until I got to the page in question. In sloppy black ballpoint pen, it said, "TO JACKIE, YOUR'S SINCERLEY, MARLYIN MONROE'. Ray's handiwork? I couldn't be sure, but I had my suspicions.

'No good?' asked Ray, smiling coyly at the expression on my face.

I was thinking about the two-hour journey back, the retracing of my wasted steps. I thought of all the trips home from Christie's and Bonhams with Margaret Rutherford or Diana Dors in my bag – never Marilyn. It seemed I never went home with Marilyn.

'Looks nothing like her autograph,' I grumbled. 'Her name isn't even spelt correctly.'

'Aw, sorry,' said Ray. 'Thought it was the real thing.'

'Sorry,' he said again, standing in his doorway, waving. 'Oh, and say hello to Dad.'

§

I woke one Sunday morning to find a rerun of the Royal Wedding on television. That was odd. Then it turned out something horrible had happened in a tunnel in Paris. How was that possible? Of all the people to die. And yet, things had been getting out of control for a while, hadn't they?

Wasn't there a new boyfriend? Hadn't she been sunning herself on a yacht with Mohamed Al-Fayed's son? There'd been that interview with the doe eyes. She'd turned out to be beautiful *and* complex, and how brave to do that – stick the knife in on prime-time TV. Then came the thought: so, if we knew how unhappy she was, how come none of us intervened? We flicked the pages of the tabloids, instead. And now the whole country was going into meltdown. It seemed everyone was struggling with their guilt. Elton John felt so bad, he refashioned his 'Candle in the Wind'.

My phone rang off the hook with requests. It was Diana they wanted now, the Americans, not Marilyn. What could I get hold of? As it turned out, I'd had a phone call from one of Diana's old chauffeurs. He had a signed Christmas card he'd consider selling for £1,000. The deal was done. I sold it for £3,000; worth just £300 days earlier. *What is it about Diana?* I mused, staring at the crowds of well-wishers on my TV screen, lining the Hendon Way to grab a final glimpse of the funeral cortège. I supposed it had taken her death to wake us all up to how much we loved her – the princess of our hearts. I certainly knew I loved her, more than ever; my biggest sale to date for a single autograph.

The news report cut to the shot outside Kensington Palace, the people laying wreathes, blowing noses, shaking heads, taking photos. Then the camera panned back to reveal the full telling scene: a mournful, glistening mountain of bouquets at the palace entrance, each one still in its own cellophane wrapper.

ELVIS

I've never written a song in my life.
It's all a big hoax.

Elvis Presley

Rachel and I were twenty-three. We managed to buy a two-bedroom flat in Willesden Green – tiny deposit, humungous interest-only mortgage. It had high ceilings, a country kitchen and its own small garden. The flat above contained a dentist/dental assistant husband-and-wife team. He was particularly short and she was particularly tall. They invited us to the local Greek restaurant, then subsequently to another Greek further afield, with wiggly dancing in between courses. Next door had three miserable children with rhyming names and two parents who shouted at them.

We arrived with our mattress and two cats, and my new credit card permitted a slow trickle of furniture. We kept the walls bare for the moment, having no idea where to start with those. We had nothing to commemorate was the problem, and we didn't want to jinx the future with false promises.

I set up my business in the second bedroom, muting the phone every night to block out the Americans. As the youngest dealer on the block, I was making an impression these days. There was a cuteness to a young guy like me with an encyclopaedic knowledge of the golden era of cinema. I started to make a bit of a name for myself as an authenticator, too. I impressed with my knowledge: for example, knowing that John Lennon carried a red biro with him everywhere he went in 1963, or that Mahatma Gandhi wrote with his left hand during 1931 because of a pain in his right thumb.

I started to get a feel, too, for the kinds of inscriptions the famous people wrote, the size of their autographs, the way they positioned their names. The trick was to look carefully at the handwriting and imagine *myself* as that celebrity. If I could conjure to mind the essence of that person, I could feel my way to the authentic – at least, I was pretty sure I could. I'd ask myself, would Andy Warhol do that particular artful flick? Would he position his autograph right there across Mao's face? Not the Andy I knew. And then there were the obvious forgery tells to look out for – if the writing was too slow, for instance, if it looked flat or lifeless, or if the ink came to a lot of unnatural stops.

Six months in, and our flat was coming together. At weekends, Rachel and I made trips to the cheap furniture store next door to Heal's on Tottenham Court Road. We came back with display pedestals made in Taiwan which we then displayed shells on retained from our childhoods. Or we bought colourful china platters that caused us to cook Middle Eastern-inspired dishes. The fax machine whirred. The bargains from eBay flowed. The walls remained bare.

And then Adrian dropped a bomb. He phoned with "exciting" news. He'd decided to buy a flat of his own. In Hampstead Village. A stone's throw from the Heath, with sole use of a large back garden. A great buy. An investment!

§

'The very worst thing was when we got evicted – did I tell you?'

Adrian asked this as he disappeared into the kitchen area of his new basement flat.

'Do you take sugar, Doobs? I've forgotten.'

'Not since I was eight,' I replied.

With Adrian out of sight, I could properly pass my eye around this pad of his. I half stood to snatch a peak at the double bed in the adjoining bedroom, then sat back down to take in the freshly upholstered sofas, gold standard lamps, Heal's coffee table. Above the fireplace a ledge was crammed with photographs; a veritable shrine. Grainy old images of people I'd not known, Grandma Lily through the ages, my father on the day of his bar mitzvah, me on the day of mine, various costumed shots of later-period Adrian, on stage, performing to his fans at Isracli dance extravaganzas. The walls were crowded with framed pictures from the house in Pinner – things I remembered my mother disliking: kitsch, multi-coloured images of synagogues, a stark Beryl Cook print of two obese women in stilettos, a simple ink caricature of two Hassidim praying. Oh, and a new inexplicable item: a large, black-and-white photograph of a snowy day in upstate New York. How did that fit it into the collection? Was my father now reimagining himself as James Stewart in *It's a Wonderful Life*, pleading with God for a second chance?

He went to great lengths, Adrian, to reassure me that the purchase of this flat did not mean he'd given up on working things out with my mother. Not remotely. It just didn't make sense to keep on paying out rent for the Regent's Park place. That was like throwing money away. Maybe – who knew – my mother would end up moving into this place with him. Or he might end up moving back to Pinner; you couldn't discount that possibility.

Adrian reappeared holding two mugs. He clambered back onto the sofa opposite me, like a student bunking off lectures.

'My parents couldn't afford the new rates when they came in,' he continued, 'so they kicked us out, and we had to be rehoused. The only place we could find was a condemned building – completely falling to pieces. The doorway from the kitchen was really just a flap in the wall that led to a staircase, with two small bedrooms upstairs – one for my parents, the other for my grandmother. The toilet was outside, and you had to walk all the way round to get to it. It was terrible in the winter, because my father was suffering with Parkinson's, so had trouble walking. He fell a couple of times. It was awful. My bedroom was right next to the kitchen. It was the only room where you could fit a television, so the whole family used it as a lounge. My parents and grandmother would sit on my bed, although never all at the same time. You see, my grandmother hated my dad. She called him a louse bag. If he was nearby, she'd mutter in Yiddish, "He should get cancer and die" or "You can do better than him, Lily" – that kind of thing. And my mother joined in – they ganged up on him. At night, my parents had terrible rows. I used to climb into their bed to get between them and stop them fighting. My mother was vicious. She had these long nails she scratched my father with. But the worst thing was when we got flooded. I came back from school one day and the whole ceiling had come in. My bedroom was filled with water, right up to the top of my mattress. The family photos that were kept in my wardrobe, the memories of happier times, they were all floating around the room – ruined.'

'Photos?'

I wondered for a moment which photos, exactly, had been ruined. I thought of the three or four I'd seen of his father; perhaps the only ones that survived.

'Not so long after that, my dad went to hospital and, of course, died there. That was a terrible shock. He had pneumonia, but I never thought he was going to die. I'd just turned nineteen.'

'I know,' I said. 'Poor you.'

It was difficult at this moment to begrudge Adrian this flat, this strange new life of his, this chance to be young again. But something still twisted in my gut, because he always had his "sad childhood" to fall back on, didn't he? His difficult early period. Always had that ace up his sleeve. And these stories about evictions and floods, just right now – was that an attempt to manipulate, a way to distract me from my anger? Not consciously, maybe. But here we were: his son visiting him in his new bachelor pad, with that son's mother abandoned in Pinner, and what were we discussing? Not the facts on the ground. Floods. Dead fathers. Mothers with clawing fingernails. What else could I do but feel pity?

'I certainly never could have imagined anything like this, back then,' he said, smiling to himself twitchily, meaning this investment opportunity in the heart of Hampstead, in the centre of everything.

'Ooh, Doobs, can I quickly show you a skit I'm planning for the dance camp?' Adrian suddenly jumped up from the sofa. 'It won't take long.'

'Sure,' I said, shrugging my arms open.

Why not, I thought? We're just two guys chewing the fat.

Adrian disappeared into his new bedroom. I could hear the wardrobes opening and slamming. A minute later, out he came, fully dressed as a Hassid: false beard, fur-rimmed shtreimel and a long black coat. He strode over to his hi-fi and got Little Richard's 'Good Golly, Miss Molly' going at considerable volume. He started his jerky sixties dancing, strolling backwards and forwards and throwing his arms out.

And then – I pinched myself – it was not a dream – while he danced, this Hassid-father of mine began exaggerated, stylized lip-synching to Little Richard.

When he'd finished, I said, 'I honestly think that might be the most cutting-edge thing I've ever seen.'

'So, you like it?' Adrian asked.

'It's special,' I said.

Adrian looked flummoxed, anxious; all comedy drained away. I took in the plaintive expression, the desperate seeking of filial approval.

'But, Doobs, you really think this'll work?'

§

I bought a signed photo of Elvis Presley on eBay from a Swedish guy – very reasonable. He contacted me directly to see if I might be interested in more. He had a trove of other signed items, all bought from the same woman in Germany, a Mrs Schneider. Elvis had stayed at this woman's house during his time in the military, and they became lifelong friends. The provenance was rock solid. One of the items on offer was a page of handwritten lyrics for a song never recorded called 'I'll Remember'. £2,000. I bought it, plus a dozen other items, all reasonably priced. They arrived in perfect condition. The lyrics were written in blue fountain pen ink, with a few crossings-out all in the King's hand. His recognizable loopy signature appeared at the bottom.

'I always loved Elvis,' Rachel said, more interested in the handsome photos I'd bought than any of the signatures. 'So charismatic. Him and John Travolta. John Travolta was my first ever crush.'

*

I took all the Elvis stuff to a trade fair in New York and stormed it. The very first item I sold was the set of lyrics. An American dealer paid me $8,000 thirty seconds after walking in through the door. Good; I could now pay off the last part of my grandfather's loan. Then all the middle-aged collectors hunched over my stall and fought for the photos.

'I like this one 'cause you don't often see him in full leather,' one buyer with long sideburns explained. 'Not signed, I don't mean. That there's from the *Comeback Special*. But you're sure of the signature? I know you've got a good eye.'

'That's Elvis alright,' I said. 'It's got the flow. Definitely his hand. And it comes with great provenance. That's the first full-leather shot of Elvis I've ever seen.'

'Interesting. I'm tempted,' said the buyer, placing his hands on his waist. 'Very tempted.'

'That's the seventy-two show at Madison Square Gardens,' said another buyer, pointing at Elvis's white jumpsuit. 'I was at that concert. That's why I'm buying it.'

'Good for you,' I said. 'Nice to have that personal connection to an item.'

'He used to dress up as a police officer,' said a third. This collector was unshaven and wearing scruffy jeans that didn't fit; he cut the look of a dodgy caretaker. 'Used to pull people over – women, mostly – and give 'em a ticket – say "You're welcome." Welcome for what? A ticket? That's Elvis for you.'

'I've heard some other strange stories about Elvis,' I tried, 'like he had a pet chimp. And ate peanut and banana sandwiches.'

'Well, I don't know nothing about that,' said the collector, blankly, perhaps offended. 'He's still alive, you know.'

'Excuse me?'

The man set his milky, swimming eyes on me and breathed, 'Elvis is alive. In South America. Venezuela. He lives at the top of a mountain, which has an elevator going all the way up. Thing is, it only operates from the top, so you can't get up there unless Elvis invites you. That's what I heard, anyway. Look, I'm interested in this photo where he's holding his guitar. That's the shot I like. That's the King. How much is it?'

A German colleague, Kurt Schmidt, was exhibiting at the same fair, staying at the same hotel as me. We met for evening drinks. It turned out he'd sold a few Presleys of his own that day.

'I sold four,' he announced, pulling his most flabbergasted face. 'Elvis is really hot right now. I've sold completely out.'

'What is it with Elvis?' I asked.

'I have no idea, but he's so easy to sell,' said Kurt. 'I can't explain his appeal if that's what you mean. I like a few of his songs but I don't see the big deal. Some of these buyers are pretty weird.'

'They are weird,' I concurred, 'but they're also putty in our hands. That's got to be my most successful autograph show yet.'

The moment I returned from New York, I sent another email to my Swedish contact. Did he have any more for sale? Any more lyrics? Several more purchases followed: a bunch of excellent signed photographs with long inscriptions to that same German friend, Mrs Schneider. A concert brochure signed on every page – ten signatures on one item. And, the pièce de résistance, a souvenir handwritten page of lyrics to

'Blue Suede Shoes'. £3,000. I'd never seen anything like it. Sold. I sent a bank transfer and waited for my treasure to arrive. When it did, I immediately contacted the American who'd bought the first set of lyrics at the fair. He bought the second right away for $12,000.

§

'He's not who I thought he was,' said my mother, ruminating over her situation in the lounge in Pinner.

The house was looking much tidier now that my father had moved out; all his hysteria expunged from the décor, the piles of postcards and heaped auction catalogues replaced by my mother's sculptures, the rabbis on the wall replaced by watercolours of Icelandic landscapes.

'Do you remember how he drove all those Russian girls around London,' continued my mother, 'giving them night-time tours of Westminster?'

'I've tried to forget,' I said.

'They wanted visas, I suppose. And all that stroking of his secretaries' cheeks? What was that about? I don't know. It's been some kind of protracted midlife crisis. He turned into someone unrecognizable – so wound up and fidgety. He honestly seemed quite normal when I first met him. Nothing but a nice boy-next-door type. I think I must have felt sorry for him because his home life was so impoverished. And when he lost his father, that sealed the deal. I must have been attracted to someone who needed taking care of.'

'That's not enough, though, is it? Feeling sorry for someone?'

'It wasn't just that. He was very loving and charming too. Everyone liked him. And he adored me in a way my parents never did – really accepted me. Look, maybe he'll sort himself out and become more normal again. Maybe this couples counselling will help, plus his own therapy.'

I thought about the mantra my father had repeated about needing to give a bit more thought to what *he* wanted. I thought about the black-and-white photograph of snowy upstate New York. I thought about the investment opportunity in the heart of Hampstead, the Heal's coffee table.

'I don't know,' I said. 'I wouldn't hold your breath.'

§

I exhibited at another trade show in Washington DC. Again, I had a good selection of Elvis in tow, courtesy of my Swedish source. While I was setting up my stall, that same American dealer came over and shook my hand.

'Adam, we have to talk about the Elvis autographs – those lyrics you sold me.'

'Sure,' I said. 'Is there a problem?'

'Well, yes. The problem is they're fake.'

The dealer locked eyes with me. My stomach descended to my feet.

'Fake? How do you mean?'

'They're forged. I've looked into it with some other dealers. It seems there's a forgery ring operating in Europe. Someone's doing these Elvises really well. They bake them in the oven to make the paper look old and use other tricks too. But it's all baloney. This Mrs Schneider – the woman Elvis was meant to have stayed with – she never existed.'

'Right,' I said. 'Are you sure?' My throat was starting to tighten.

'I wish I wasn't. There's a guy in Sweden selling all these

on behalf of another guy in Austria, and that guy in Austria is the rock 'n' roll expert for some of the big London auction houses. This thing goes really deep. Take another look at them and compare them to authentic examples. There are some tells there. You'll see what I mean when you look. The 'P' of Presley is too flat on top. The writing's too slow.'

'I'll take a proper look,' I said. 'I'm shocked to hear all this.'

'So, look, Adam, I'll need to return the two lyrics to you for a refund. I'm sure you understand. And you'll need to contact your other buyers. This thing will blow up in your face, otherwise.'

The refunds totalled £30,000, and my Swedish contact wasn't responding to the emails I was sending from my hotel room. I remembered that I'd paid him by bank transfer, which meant the money was now irretrievable.

Kurt Schmidt commiserated with me at the airport. He could see how tough it was going to be for me to manage my cash flow.

'It was too good to be true,' I said. 'The items got better and better. Who could turn them down at those prices? But, a souvenir copy of 'Blue Suede Shoes'? How could I have been so stupid?'

I felt humiliated. My authentication skills had let me down. It hadn't been Elvis at all. It had been a greedy Austrian. Maybe I'd been greedy, too? I called to mind those times seasoned autograph dealers had said to me, *If it seems too good to be true, then it's probably not true.*

'I guess it's a learning experience,' said Kurt. 'Next time you'll see the warning signs. Once bitten, twice shy. Why don't you let me look through your binders?' he suggested. 'Maybe I can buy a few things to help you out.'

He bought a lot – at cost price. He bought signed photos of Walt Disney, Charlie Chaplin, Humphrey Bogart and Neil Armstrong. He inserted them into his hand luggage and shook my hand goodbye.

§

'Amazing,' said Adrian. 'I mean, awful for you, awful you have to refund everything. But amazing that the forgeries were so good, and the paper looked so old. And to think that the guy doing them authenticates for auction houses.'

'I'm taking a big hit,' I said, 'and I never want to see Elvis's face again.'

Adrian smiled, then said, 'You do know that Elvis and I share a birthday?'

They did? I had no idea. How weird. I figured I had to have known an odd little piece of information like that; I had to have known it and forgotten.

We took a walk down Hampstead High Street and Adrian started up on one of his speeches about the joys of living in NW3. He said everywhere he looked he saw people he wanted to talk to. He said he felt like he was right in the centre of things. His walk was honestly more of a swagger, as if he was hoping he might be noticed and stopped by one of his Israeli dance fans – remembered for the ventriloquism act, or the blind circumcision. The shopkeepers in Flask Walk knew him by name. They waved as we passed, or stopped him to offer updates on sick in-laws. Adrian pinched his lips together and nodded sympathetically.

Then his phone rang. He turned his back on me and covered the receiver with both hands.

I wondered who it was. The woman from Israeli dancing that my mother had heard so much about?

Adrian quickly ended the call and smiled into the sunshine.

'How's Mummy, by the way? Have you spoken to her recently? Is she coping?'

'She's *coping*,' I said, guardedly. 'I wouldn't say she's having the time of her life.'

'Yes, well, it's strange for me too, Doobs. It really is. I never in a million years imagined myself ending up in this situation. I'm very torn, actually. Part of me really does want to work things out, and yet another part of me just isn't sure it's right to go back. Look, we'll see. We'll see what happens.'

We'll see what happens? I'd heard that line somewhere before. In a bedsit opposite Regent's Park Mosque, after he'd moved out of the house in Pinner. One of Adrian's tells! Because things indeed had "happened" since then. He'd bought a flat in Hampstead! I thought of saying nothing, then remembered what Kurt Schmidt had said to me in the departure lounge at Washington airport. Once bitten, twice shy.

'Look, Dad, when you say, "we'll see", what do you mean, exactly?'

My face was burning up. For once, I could feel my hackles rising. I was angry, despite the sad childhood and the ceiling that caved in, despite the fingernails and the father who fell over and died. I was being had.

'I mean, you've bought yourself a new flat, haven't you, Dad? It's pretty clear to anyone with half a brain you've already started a new life.'

'It was a good buy,' said Adrian. 'That's why I bought it. It made no sense to keep on paying out rent.'

'Yes, you've said that. But you're not honestly planning to move back to Pinner, are you? You've clearly made a decision.'

My father stood still, a look of surprise plastered over his face.

'You've moved on with your life, Dad,' I continued. 'And now you need to come clean with Mum. You can't keep her hanging on. It's not fair. You have to tell her!'

HITLER

Will the dancing Hitlers please wait
in the wings? We are only seeing
singing Hitlers.

'Roger De Bris', in *The Producer*s

Adrian confessed. He was involved with an Italian woman; a Catholic with a deep love of Israeli dancing. She was thirty-two years old – twenty-two years his junior – five years older than my sister. It was love. My mother began divorce proceedings.

I joined for the first meeting with the lawyer, at offices in Westminster; all sombre handshakes and nods. My mother burst into tears, went over everything that had happened, quite forgot the £300 per hour fee. She talked about Adrian's troubled childhood, his impossible mother, his need to entertain. I interjected a bit about his rise to great heights on the Israeli dance scene. Then we got on to his synagogues.

'It's just vanity,' Mum explained, 'in the guise of preserving history. It's about him being the centre of attention.'

I shuffled in my seat, thinking about my lifelong fascination with the famous, my own meteoric rise in the autograph industry.

'I don't know,' concluded my mother, shaking her head. 'Things have been strange for a long time.'

The lawyer returned a blank look of professional concern, tapped a tidy pile of folders on his desk, then interlinked his fingers.

'I should have seen it coming,' continued my mother.

'But you did, didn't you?' I said. Then, with a clunk of resignation, 'We all did.'

It was the lawyer's turn to speak now. His voice was melty

and hypnotic. He moved his eyes back and forth between my mother and me as if we were an exquisite pair of ornate antique vases. We were both nodding profusely even before the lawyer finished his first sentence.

In his opinion, the best thing we could now do was put the whole thing into his hands. Divorce was a difficult process for everyone involved, and a neutral third party was by far the best way to settle such disputes. The lawyer assured us he was the very best at what he did – he was thorough, wouldn't leave a stone unturned and would guide the whole thing to a logical and satisfactory conclusion. He opened one of his folders as he spoke, and I caught a glimpse of a dense page of numbers in ledger format. I wondered if he'd already turned my parents into a maths equation: Adrian's numbers on one side, Anna's on the other. Good times and bad times converted to algebra. If anyone had bothered to keep a tally of my father's best jokes over the years, that could now be deducted from the number of nights my mother sat at home, dinner getting cold, waiting for him to return from the office.

As the lawyer talked on, I had the uncanny feeling we were being subsumed into a giant system, that we would lose our foothold once the enormous corporate wheels were set in motion. I imagined the minutes of this meeting typed up by some fastidious secretary, piles of papers ferried around London in black cabs, the millions of sheets, each bearing the same geometric stamp of the divorce lawyers' offices, soon to be the only tangible trace of a thirty-seven-year lived relationship.

'Oh,' said the lawyer, pursing his pink lips and smiling, 'it's probably best not to discuss anything of a financial nature with Adrian for the time being – best everything goes via me.'

§

I managed to get over the Elvis cash flow nightmare. It took some time. I sold material at cost price, sent autographs away to auction, sold a few items at a loss, but soon enough I was eking out a living again. After three or four months, business was booming. The "want lists" kept on arriving, as did the frenzied calls from clients around the world. New collectors emerged, each hungering after his own very particular flavour. The mortgage was paid. I was back on my feet.

But there was something else now. I was restless in a different way. I felt myself to be drowning in a foamy pool of rapacious Americans, several years into a career I'd never wanted. I was a dealer profiteering from other people's delusions of grandeur. I fed narcissists for a living, massaged the egos of a thousand Adrians. I couldn't help wondering what the old me would have had to say about it. *What happened to the concertos at the Festival Hall?* And, *When, exactly, do you plan on etching your greatness into the world?* I needed to rethink things. I was sleepwalking in the wrong direction. On reflection, what I needed was a divorce from autographs. Was that something the lawyers in Westminster could help with?

It was in this spirit of agitation that I attended a collectors' convention in Fort Lauderdale, Florida. I was restless and irritable. The hotel was pink and had a waterfall in the lobby. Large, elderly people crept around everywhere. My bedroom had three rooms with four chairs and two tables. Outside was a motorway. I lay back on my bouncy castle and flicked on

the television. A bombing in Kenya by a terrorist group I'd
not heard of: Al-Qaeda. Jim Carrey in *Liar, Liar.* That clip,
again, of Clinton on his "improper physical relationship". All
these garnered my interest for a second, then faded.

I flicked through my autograph binders, adding stickers
and numbers and inserting the typed descriptions that drew
attention to rarity, uniqueness, desirability. It was a routine
I'd gone through so many times before. Margaret Thatcher
and Mother Teresa shaking hands again, another NASA
8×10 of Neil Armstrong in the spacesuit, a signed colour
photograph of Ayatollah Khomeini (a flash of Adrian's old
composites, his Hassidic face grinning over the top of the
clerical outfit). DiCaprio and Winslet in the *Titanic* clinch,
Jack Nicholson as the Joker. When you'd seen a hundred of
these, the excitement waned. My career: the never-ending
treasure hunt with the same old tired prizes.

At least Kurt Schmidt was attending the show, which meant
we could eat steaks as long as our arms at the restaurant on
the other side of the hotel's football-pitch-size car park, and
gossip about the other dealers and collectors.

'I visited one collector in his house today,' said Kurt,
pushing what looked like an entire cow's flank to the side of
his plate. 'One of those guys who collects Nazi autographs.
Bill Smith – you know him?'

'No.'

'He's a weird guy. Has a large moat around his house.
Inside were framed photographs everywhere of Hitler. On
the walls in huge, gold frames. Also, a few of Einstein. In the
bathroom he had two Hitlers and a Marilyn. And in between
all those pictures were actual guns.'

'You're kidding.'

The idea of a house like that, and Kurt being in it, woke me from my lethargy. It brought up a curious mix of feelings. The most obvious was fear, followed closely by disgust. But beneath those, a tangible feeling of fascination – that a house like that could exist; that people could admire the man who murdered my family members. And buried yet deeper, a peculiar twinge of jealousy – yes, jealousy! – of the audacity, I supposed: of the wild freedom it suggested.

'It's pretty strange,' said Kurt, opening his hands. 'He bought all my Hitlers and kept saying "what a beautiful example" and grinning at me as if we're both fans of the Third Reich together.'

'Now, where could he have got that idea from?' I tried, with a smirk.

I had exhibited beside Kurt many a time, and it was only ever minutes till some American was slow-turning the pages of his Hitler & Gang binder, then pausing to surreptitiously ask the German if he ever came across any Eva Brauns or Reinhard Heydrichs? Or perhaps he'd be interested in a nice Adolf Eichmann?

'No, it's not like that,' said Kurt, looking abashed. 'I offer only a few of the bigger names. They are so easy to sell.'

'That's OK, Kurt. I know you're not a Nazi. Not an active one, anyway.'

The German dealer laughed, but I could see I was making him uncomfortable. I told him not to worry; that I was being like my father. I explained how Adrian made regular speeches about never buying a German car. Kurt looked more anxious than reassured by that revelation. And I left it there. After all, hadn't I sold a few Stalins, Francos and Gaddafis over the previous year? I'd also heard that Ayatollah Khomeini wasn't such a nice guy.

At the convention, the two guests of honour were the commander and bombardier of the *Enola Gay*. I stood at my stall with my mouth agape when the announcement was made. The two old men streamed in, to enthusiastic applause. They shook hands with all the dealers and grinned like Olympic gold medallists. That mix of fear and fascination came over me again. I turned to Kurt at the next stall.

'I'm not shaking their hands,' I said. 'Let them try.'

'I'm not so keen either,' said Kurt.

The two old men settled down at their table, where a selection of photographs of the devastation of Hiroshima were laid out in front of them. They sipped their coffees. They picked up Sharpie pens. Collectors formed a queue.

'You see that guy right there?' said Kurt, pointing to a weaselly, thin man at the front of the line holding an enormous stylized oil painting of the Hiroshima mushroom cloud under his arm. 'That's Bill Smith.'

Ha! That was him? Another display of audacity! The brazen shamelessness of it! I watched in amazement as Smith placed his oil painting on the table in front of the *Enola Gay* crew, then fielded what looked like compliments on its structure and brushwork. One of the old men signed his name across the top of the painting, the spot where you could see an image of a tilted aeroplane flying off into the distance. Smith leant forward to say something, then both old men threw back their heads in laughter.

§

Embedded back in Willesden with the auction catalogues – the lists of names, the crudely built websites. While searching for other dealers' pricing errors, I suddenly came upon a Dutch ephemera dealer offering a copy of *Mein Kampf* signed by Adolf Hitler himself in fountain pen ink, dated December 1938. Four thousand Dutch guilders – the equivalent of £1,300 – a serious steal. I made the call, and a guy with a slidey accent told me the book was available. I hesitated. I'd never bought Nazis before. I pictured the look of disgust on Adrian's face whenever he mentioned Dr Levy's collection of anti-Semitica. I remembered my father's early-morning lectures on the Final Solution. I thought of the hundred or so Hitler autographs I'd flicked past in dealers' binders over the previous few years.

'Any chance you could hold it for a few days?' I asked. I needed to think about it. I needed to consult with my conscience.

'It won't go anywhere,' said the dealer. 'Let me know either way.'

§

'So, how was the trip to Florida?' asked Adrian.

Simon and Garfunkel were blaring through the speakers at his Hampstead pad, competing with what sounded like a child practising Schumann next door. The shrine of photographs had been added to, I noticed: a new shot of my father dressed as a kosher butcher clutching a rubber chicken in each hand, and a posed shot showing a group of grinning young dancers forming a semi-circle around Adrian, shown sporting both a false Hassidic beard and a Native American headdress.

'Did you buy anything exciting, Doobs? Anything you're going to keep?'

'Well, I don't really keep things any more,' I sighed. Only the twentieth time I'd told him. *And I don't take sugar in my tea*, I wanted to add.

'Well, I must just show you a few things *I've* recently bought.'

Adrian disappeared off into his bedroom, lithe, light on his feet, while I collapsed on the sofa, taking the weight off mine. With the divorce in progress, my mother was never far from my thoughts, and when I visited the Hampstead pad I felt particularly guilty – as if I was inadvertently endorsing my father's new lifestyle. The crystalline photograph of the snowy day in upstate New York caught my eye again, plus a new signed photograph of Rudolf Nureyev and Margot Fonteyn. Since when did my father collect autographs?

'Some of these cards are very important,' Adrian announced, returning with a padded envelope. 'These are all Polish synagogues that were destroyed by the Nazis. Some I've never seen before. These are an important historical record. Very rare. Look.'

Adrian began turning black-and-white postcards in his hand, lingering on each image for a number of seconds of his choosing, and shaking his head. Interspersed with the images of synagogues were photographs of various Jewish people – in rows at long dinner tables, in group youth club poses, lined up outside kosher shops. Photographs of people who had no idea what was going to happen to them.

'These cards are highly sought after,' said Adrian. 'I know several collectors who'd kill to have them. Dr Levy, for example. To think that these people all perished. Just terrible.

You see, Doobs, when Hitler invaded Poland, all the Jews in these towns were moved to the Łódź ghetto, then on to Auschwitz. These synagogues were destroyed. The Nazis were such bastards.'

Adrian turned to me, offering his smouldering, poignant face, and I returned mine. The images were terribly sad. The story was painful, no matter how old it got. But then I found myself asking an age-old companion question: what was it about my father and the Holocaust? Why was this his subject?

'How's Mummy, by the way?' Adrian flicked a smile, blinked his eyes a lot.

The clunk in my stomach, the twist in my gut. I thought of the tears at the lawyer's office, the eternal soul-searching.

'She's . . . fine, I guess.'

'I only hear from her through lawyers now, which is a shame,' said Adrian, 'because I really do miss her. Honestly! I still love her, you know, Doobs. Of course, I do. That hasn't changed. It never will. I just think it would have been so much simpler if we could have worked things out between us without involving all these lawyers, but that's up to Mummy. I'll do whatever she wants. Anyway, I'm glad she's fine. Is she seeing friends?'

'Yes. She sees friends.'

'Good. That's important. It's not good to be alone. Ooh, now I must just show you another amazing photograph. It's very upsetting, but interesting – an interesting record.'

He was up again, with the spring in his step.

And then I thought, my God, it's the same trick again! The sleight of hand! If it's not dead fathers and floods and mothers with clawing fingernails, it's destroyed synagogues and the Nazi Killing Machine. Cheating husbands? Family treachery? When exactly would we alight upon those topics?

'You know what, Dad, I think I've had enough for now. I don't want to see any more.'

When I got back to my flat, I decided that was it: I was buying Hitler. I was buying Hitler if it was the last thing I did. I rang the dealer in the Netherlands and rattled off my credit card number. A few days later the package arrived. Unwrapping it caused a strange thrill, and there was an even greater one when I took into my hands the volume of *Mein Kampf*. I flipped open the book and there it was: Adolf Hitler's signature. He had placed his hand on this very page. There had to be tiny molecules of him lurking. I touched the signature, moved my fingers across its grooves in the paper. I knew it was authentic, could feel the unmistakable pulse and speed of Adolf.

I wondered how appalled Adrian would be about this, a thought that released a whole pile of endorphins. Then I wondered what Hitler would think about being used by a Jew to get one up on another Jew. That felt more complicated. But, then, Hitler wasn't the point, was he? Not really. Not the actual man. Now that I owned this signature, now that I'd broken the taboo, I could see the Führer for who he really was. My Hitler was a ridiculous, thin-skinned madman with a penchant for camp clothing. A bad painter who couldn't take the flak. Nothing like the gun-toting one on Bill Smith's walls.

I wore my Hitler autograph as a badge of honour for some time.

'I've something disturbing to show you,' I said, with relish, to anyone who set foot in our flat. Then I retrieved my Hitler from the top of the piano, where I kept it stashed, and back I flounced.

Rachel looked on uncertainly, each time, as I excitedly turned to the title page and revealed Adolf's spindly signature.

'There he is. That's him.'

I'd slam it shut again, exercising total control over the dictator. The guest would offer a crooked smile, a look of bafflement, and Rachel would look exasperated; just the exact same expression my mother used to have when Adrian harped on about Treblinka during episodes of *'Allo 'Allo!*

§

Back in the consulting room with my Australian therapist, and I was in good spirits. He'd been told all about the triumph of *Mein Kampf*, how I'd separated from my father once and for all, dared to break the taboo. I was free, just like the guy in Florida with the moat around his house.

The Australian smiled but wasn't saying much. I wondered if maybe Hitler wasn't his area.

'I guess I'm wondering, is it really that simple?' he said, eventually. 'What I mean is, do you think collecting Nazi memorabilia is the right way to process your anger with your father? I mean, if it is, you've clearly struck gold.'

§

Kurt Schmidt asked me to collect an item for him from Christie's auction house in London. He'd bought one of Sigmund Freud's own walking sticks and needed it shipped. It was a wooden cane with a silver curved handle.

For several weeks I kept the Freud stick under my bed, and for those weeks it felt like it was mine. It was quite something to have Hitler and Freud under one roof, not least because one had wanted to kill the other. Also, Freud, who escaped Nazi Germany in 1938, created a whole school of thought that ultimately gave succour to many of Hitler's victims and their descendants.

I had a routine I liked to perform. I held Hitler in one hand and Freud in the other. It was like an axis of good and evil, as if I was weighing up two competing parts of my soul. For a while now, I'd been experiencing a growing sense of guilt at owning Hitler, and Freud was now helping to assuage it.

'Enjoying Hitler and Freud again?' asked Rachel. 'That's nice. Very Freudian.'

'Yes, but I'm worried,' I said, 'that my Hitler isn't going to feel quite the same without Freud. I've got used to it. And now Kurt wants me to ship the walking stick out to him this week. So, maybe it's finally time for me to sell *Mein Kampf*.'

'No kidding,' said Rachel. 'We really don't need to have Nazis living with us. If you want to upset your dad, why don't you just buy a German car?'

I shipped Hitler away to auction. Freud was FedExed to Germany. From there, knowing Kurt Schmidt, it was sent on to Fort Lauderdale to a certain house with a moat. I've often pictured the stick nestled between portraits of Adolf Hitler, opposite the Hiroshima mushroom cloud, perched above a highly sought-after pair of original World War Two Mauser M712 Schnellfeuer guns.

MONICA LEWINSKY

Monica's Story

· ·

ANDREW MORTON

Michael O'Mara Books Limited

I'm kind of known for something
that's not so great to be known for.

Monica Lewinsky turning down
an autograph request

All I knew about Adrian's girlfriend, apart from her age and predilection for Israeli folk dancing, was that she was Italian and a child psychologist. The profession suggested to me that my father had bagged her by citing his "sad childhood". The nationality implied an insurmountable language barrier at the heart of their love affair.

'All I know is she's had her eye on him for some time,' said Mum, stirring the teapot in Pinner. 'She must have father issues. She made a beeline for him – made a decision and got her clutches in.'

'Well, we don't know that for sure,' I said. 'I mean, we don't know Dad was that passive.'

'According to the person I spoke to,' continued my mother, 'this *woman* was staring into Adrian's eyes very creepily while they danced. I'm telling you, she made a decision. She's had trouble finding anyone her own age, I expect. Next thing, she'll want a baby. You're not going to actually meet this person, are you?'

'Well, I don't have plans to,' I said, 'although, at some point, I guess I'll have to. I don't know. Can't say I'm keen.'

A look of concern settled on my mother's face as she looked out at the garden, at the one unchanged view still available to her. The pond, the apple tree, the gentle upward slope of the lawn between the two cypress trees. That view was etched into my retina too, and I took it in greedily, a panacea to all this madness. I looked around the lounge again, at how completely and spookily reorganized it had been. The divorce was done and dusted, the paper trail at an end, and not one trace left of Adrian. It was all Anna now.

'Don't forget to take the photos with you,' said my mother, still gazing out of the big window, her voice thin and remote. 'I don't see why I should be the custodian of everyone's past.'

She meant the pictures from my childhood, the dozens of photo albums filled with thousands of blurred, haphazard snapshots taken by my father in the 1980s. She'd put them in plastic bags by the front door.

'I'll take them,' I said. 'That's fine.'

'But what can she *be* like?' I pleaded with Rachel. 'I mean, what on earth made her fall for my dad? When she turns fifty, he'll be seventy-two. It's weird. Can it be about security? He doesn't have much money.'

'You should probably meet her,' said Rachel. 'It'll drive you mad, otherwise – the not knowing.'

'I can't very well do that, though, can I? That would be like giving him my blessing. So awful for my mum. I'd feel guilty. I tell you what, I bet my dad gave her a whole sob story about the wife that didn't understand him, the wife who didn't like Israeli dancing. Maybe this Italian woman took pity on him.'

'Well, unless you meet her, Adam, it's all guesswork, isn't it?'

I visited my 86-year-old grandfather and discovered he was more concerned about JFK, these days, than my parents' divorce.

'I became very disillusioned lately,' he said, glowering at

me across his kitchen table. 'It turns out Kennedy was a womanizer. A different girl in every city. I saw a programme. And I got so sickened by what I heard that I slung his book in the bin.'

He was referring to the enormous volume of *A Thousand Days in the White House*, which had enjoyed pride of place on his bookshelf for three decades.

'You threw away a book, Grandpa?'

I smiled at the idea, but there was no flicker of humour on the old man's face.

'I had such a high opinion of him, but I changed my mind completely. And, as for your father, as for Adrian, well . . . I'm not pleased about what happened there, either.' Grandpa Jožka tilted his head and widened his eyes, then added, 'But, on the other hand, you never really know what goes on between people.'

'That's true, I suppose.'

My grandfather tapped his fingers together and sighed.

'It can be about sex, actually,' he mused. 'You see, Addie, marriage is not always so easy. It's not a bed of roses. When a woman gets older, she loses interest. It can be very difficult.'

I shifted uneasily on my seat, trying not to think about my parents and sex, also trying not to think about my grandfather's new girlfriend, Zdenka, a frightening-looking woman with bony cheeks and wild, starey eyes. She didn't speak a word of English, but her clipped, dismissive manner told you everything you needed to know. God knows, she didn't look like she'd lost interest.

When she was introduced to my grandfather by mutual friends in Prague, it turned out the two already knew

each other. They had met decades earlier when my grandfather's army division had liberated Zdenka's town in
Czechoslovakia. She'd been fifteen years old at that time. In
the restaurant in Prague she produced her diary from 1945,
which included a little love sonnet in Jožka's hand.
1945, when my grandfather was happily married to my
grandmother and had a two-year-old son in England. ('Oh,
just a kiss and a cuddle – nothing more,' he explained to my
perturbed mother.)

Since their Prague reunion, Jožka had taken Zdenka on
several of the exact holidays he'd enjoyed with my grandmother. He'd taken her to many of the restaurants they'd
frequented. He even twice forced the Czech-speaker to sit
through his and my grandmother's favourite film, *Moon-
struck*. What she made of it was anyone's guess. He was
candid about the gap in his life being filled by this woman.
'I'm lonely,' he said, 'and it's nothing intense. She stays there
in Prague. Just a few holidays together each year.' I didn't
begrudge him this new relationship – not at all – but it hadn't
been easy for my mother. 'She looks like a pantomime dame,'
she'd commented, after clapping her eyes on Zdenka for the
first time.

'Now, my grandson, how is business?'

'Pretty good,' I said. 'I'm moving into higher-end
material. Getting away from entertainment – dealing mainly
in autograph letters. Some of them have amazing content.
I recently sold a Gandhi letter written from prison, and a
whole Einstein correspondence.'

'Really?' A big smile spread across my grandfather's face.
'What a k'nacker. My grandson, the entrepreneur. Just like

I was at your age. But how you started up your business is amazing. No apprenticeship, nothing. You just decided to do it.'

'Well, I guess. My father was a collector, though, don't forget. I'm sure that must have been part of it.'

'Yes, but he collects these pictures of synagogues.' A sour, dismissive expression twisted across my grandfather's face. 'I don't know why he wants such things. He's not religious. And the Holocaust is not even a part of his history. Very strange.'

'I don't know, Grandpa,' I said. 'Maybe it's just a way of him avoiding his own personal trauma. I mean his childhood.' I thought fleetingly about the fights between his parents, the police being called, the family photos floating in floodwater.

My grandfather screwed up his eyes with impatience and swatted away my analysis with his hand. 'But what you found,' he continued, 'is such a big field – all these historical letters, as you say. I had no idea about such a trade. Very clever of you.'

'Thanks, Grandpa.'

'Ach. You know who was also clever?'

'Who?'

'My mother.' Grandpa Jožka took a deep breath and closed his eyes as he exhaled. 'I think about her such a lot. Every day I see her face. Ach, it's no good talking.' He wiped the corner of his eye, then leant his arms on the table. 'And how is your darling? How is Rachel? Please, Addie, when will you get married?'

'I don't know, Grandpa. I'm only twenty-five. There's no great rush, is there?'

'For you, maybe not, but *I'm* in a rush. I want you to have a baby. I want to be alive to see it!'

§

It was true that I'd moved into autograph letters of historical importance, but when Movie Guy mentioned he'd be attending a book signing by Monica Lewinsky, it piqued my interest. I remembered a signed card by Bill Clinton lurking somewhere in my cupboard. It was worth $200, but what if I could get Lewinsky to sign the same card? That could be worth thousands. I found the autograph, and to my delight Clinton's signature was written quite far up on the card, which left a large space underneath it just for Monica. I couldn't resist the opportunity.

I told Movie Guy I would meet him at Harrods, then set about cunningly hiding the Clinton signature from view. It was highly unlikely Lewinsky would agree to sign alongside the president, so I created a cardboard matte that completely covered his signature, leaving just a small white box. I made a large space above where I inserted a picture of Monica. So, what it looked like was a photo of Lewinsky with a white blank space below, ready to be signed. Not one of my finest moments.

Harrods was mayhem. People jostled for position to ensure a good line of vision. This was the woman who'd had the presidential appendage in her mouth, after all. We'd all heard the blowjob and semen jokes. We wanted to see her. It was a new kind of fame. Movie Guy's bald head was sweating.

Lewinsky entered, stage left, looking pretty and breezy. All eyes were on her. A woman behind me tutted and muttered, 'Look at that. Not a flicker of shame.' Monica started signing books, smiling up at each person in turn. Her eyes were sparkly. I felt uneasy as I neared the front of the queue, the obligatory copy of *Monica's Story* under my right arm, the ridiculous matted up Lewinsky tribute under my left.

'I'd really like you to sign *here*, if possible,' I said to Monica, standing at her desk and pointing down to the white space I'd manufactured beneath her image.

She took in the weird object before her and narrowed her eyes suspiciously. Then she offered me a look of apology.

'Sorry, but I'm really only able to sign the books,' she said.

I nodded vociferously that I completely understood; understood her position entirely, understood she was too canny for a cheap trick like mine. I intuited that only one of us truly needed to feel ashamed at that moment, and it wasn't her. I'd objectified her, commodified her – just like everyone else. As I headed home with my signed book, I had a further realization: this would probably be the last autograph I would ever ask for.

§

I was with Rachel in Waterstones on Hampstead High Street, pretending to flick through a book about Prince Philip. We were here to meet my father's girlfriend. A first – definitely up there with buying my first Hitler.

'Are you OK?' asked Rachel.

'Fine,' I gibbered. 'Totally fine.'

I opened a book entitled *Embracing Defeat.* That was about right. It did feel like a surrender of sorts. I was surrendering to Adrian, wasn't I, but also to myself; agreeing to let go of a particular version of my life. I did think it was time for me to give up on trying to "solve" my parents. They were not a maths problem. They were not the Riemann hypothesis. Maybe seeing this other woman in the flesh might help me accept that some problems couldn't be solved, that one half of me didn't quite fit with the other.

And then, in she came. Beside my father stood a neat-looking individual with black hair and rectangular glasses. She offered a kindly smile and reached out to shake my hand.

'I'm Giorgia,' she said. 'Very glad to meet you.'

Her accent was strong, as was her handshake. She spoke at a confident volume, like a woman who knew herself well. Already so different to my mother, whose tone was always exploratory, apologetic, self-doubting, who carefully edited herself to conform to the sensibilities of others.

'I've been reading about how Prince Philip was born on a kitchen table in Corfu,' I bumbled.

'Really?' laughed Giorgia. 'I didn't know.'

I introduced Rachel, guiding her with my hand, careful to avoid my father's enthusiastic twitches, akin to an over-attentive waiter.

The four of us ambled out of the bookshop in an odd clump and went to sit at the Coffee Cup, a few doors down.

'Tea, Doobs?' asked my father.

'Sure.'

'And what about you, my darling?'

My father laid his hand on the shoulder of this woman

who wasn't my mother. I found I couldn't draw from my lexicon of acerbic observations, because A no longer equalled B. I couldn't read the signals between these two people. Might there be an opportunity to see my father with new eyes, then?

Giorgia touched my father's hand and said, 'I'll have a coffee, darling.'

Then we talked. We talked about northern Italy, about tea and coffee, about the way Hampstead High Street had changed over the years, about autographs.

'Ah, so it's about your expertise as an authenticator,' she interjected. 'Not everyone could do your job.'

'Exactly.'

Then we talked about her work, how she was employed by the NHS as part of a team of psychologists who dealt with families in crisis. I breathed agitatedly through that part. She described everything in the same firm, authoritative tone and answered, anticipated, my queries in a forthright manner. When my father tried to interrupt, she gently pushed him back out of the conversation.

'Adrian, hold on, I'm explaining,' she said, then she turned to touch my father gently on the arm and smiled.

I asked about Israeli dancing, how she'd got into it; because wasn't she a Catholic?

'I like all kinds of dance, actually. I used to enjoy tango. But then I found Israeli dancing, and it sort of stuck. Of course, Adrian *truly* loves it – more than me, actually – but, yes, I do enjoy it a lot.'

I noticed my father listening in, subdued into the listener's role, one of the necessary concessions, he had to be discovering, when you entitled yourself to a younger partner. He needed to stay on his toes, I sensed. Still, there were the moments when Giorgia looked at Adrian – lovingly, eyes bright – and I sensed an admiration. Early days, I thought. She's only just started investing. Part of me wanted to give her the lowdown. She ought to hear about the claustrophobic relationship with Grandma Lily, at least, surely? The late-night phone calls from the car? But another part of me was tired and wanted to lay down my weapons. If I carried on fighting this battle I'd never stop, and meanwhile life would go on all around me. I needed to remove the Adrian flavour from my life, do the trick my mother had done with the lounge.

'I know it must be incredibly hard for you to meet me,' said Giorgia, suddenly.

I could see that she'd prepared this bit, and I was glad she had.

'It's brave of you, Adam. Especially because I know you're very concerned about your mother. And the age difference must be strange. It's strange for me, actually. I never expected to meet someone your father's age. Not at all. But I'm grateful that you're giving me this chance. I don't expect anything from you. Really.'

Adrian grinned – still in the role of listener – then he gave the hand signal to the waiter for the bill.

As we made our way back up Hampstead High Street Rachel talked to Giorgia, while my father and I were thrown together for the first time.

'How's Mummy?' was the first thing he said.

Clunk. He was trying to reassure me that my mother was forever in his thoughts. Still, it produced the usual twist in my gut.

'She's fine,' I said, warding him off with my eyes, but you could never truly ward off Adrian.

'Oh, good. Good. And, Doobs, I'm very glad you've done this. It's great. Giorgia's really happy about it, and I am too.'

'But I didn't do it for you,' I said, stopping still in the street.

I felt indignant suddenly. I wasn't going to fall for any tricks. Not now.

'I'm doing it for me, Dad, so I can get on with my life. Also, for Rachel, so she doesn't have to spend the rest of hers hearing about all this shit.'

'Yes, of course, Doobs. I understand. But I'm still proud of you.'

My father walked up ahead to join Giorgia, and I found myself bristling. This wasn't at all the moment for Adrian's pride. Rachel was walking by my side now, turning to look at me, wanting to know what I thought.

'She's nice,' I said. 'What can I say? She's nice.'

I watched as my father took Giorgia's arm in his and held his head high. Like two tango dancers, I thought. He pointed at a shop window as if he'd spotted something he might buy later. He had to be relieved the meeting had gone this well. He had to be breathing a sigh of relief. He stopped still and turned towards me.

'Doobs, Giorgia's brother is keen to get hold of a signed photo of Fred Astaire,' he said. 'Maybe you can help him find one?'

Now you're pushing your luck, I thought.

'Thing is,' I said, 'I don't really deal in entertainment autographs any more.' I opened my hands in apology.

'You've still kept *some*, though, haven't you?' asked Adrian, looking shocked at such news. 'You had such a nice collection.'

He turned back again and wasn't expecting an answer, I didn't think. He didn't get it. He'd never get it. He was smiling into the sunlight now, contemplating some aspect of his future. He was likely thinking about an Israeli dance marathon. Or the next opportunity to dress as a Hassid. Or maybe something else completely that I couldn't possibly know about. But he wasn't thinking of Anna – not really. He'd bequeathed her to me now. All loose ends tied up. For a moment, I felt infuriated at the thought of my father's future freedom – undeserved, essentially – while mine forever included this marriage break-up of his, and the sadness and confusion it left behind. Plus, now that he'd thanked me, I felt dirty into the bargain, because he'd tried to take something for himself, tried to assuage his own guilt; sleight of hand. Still, at least this woman Giorgia had lost her mystery – that was a bonus. She had two eyes and a mouth. And two arms, one of which she was now detaching from my father's, to glance at her watch.

Yes, it seemed about time for me, too, if I was honest. This day was done. I also had a life to get back to – the rest of my twenties, for starters. Adrian had been in his twenties once, I reflected, but you never heard much about those years. Did they get edited out of the feature film? Or maybe he just stopped chronicling for a while. Perhaps I'd do the same.

'Come on, Rach', I said, 'let's go home.'

I shook hands with Giorgia, and she thanked me again – held my eye. But, wait. What was Adrian up to? Only fiddling in his bag, now obscuring his face with a large camera.

'This way, Doobs, Rachel,' he shouted. 'Ooh, lovely. Come on. Look at me. One more.'

EPILOGUE

Sandwiched between two dealers in 2012 – a diminutive Frenchwoman and an enormous New Yorker – in the back of a taxi, processing our way through an ornate set of open gates, then along a mile-long stretch of tiled driveway. We floated past a disused sun-streamed tennis court being hosed down by workmen, then a moss-eaten marble fountain featuring an array of horses' heads.

'Almost there,' said the New York dealer, the only one of us who actually knew the collector we were visiting.

A human-size outdoor chess board came into view, standing idle, as if a game had been abandoned there decades earlier. Then the mansion itself, which had turrets and balconies and crumbling brickwork.

'Like HMS *Victory*,' I observed, because the house seemed cocked at an angle in the middle of this vast lawned estate. A palm tree emerged from its inner courtyard like a gigantic mast.

The New York dealer took out a handkerchief and pulled it across his sweaty brow, then caught sight of something in the mid-distance and hastily put it back in his pocket.

'Heeere's Johnny!' he roared.

I spotted the elderly collector silhouetted against the mansion's doorway, a man of about eighty, of Iranian descent – Yohannan Razi. The captain of the ship.

He had tight curls dyed black and was wearing a white polo neck, gold medallion, shabby jeans and a look of habitual distrust. I supposed that was fair enough, because Razi had never in fact met two of us dealers before. Still, when we decamped from the taxi, at the exact moment I produced my hand for shaking, he turned his back and beckoned us inside, as if we were here to renovate a plunge pool or stair-lift, rather than seal a long and complicated deal to buy his Nelson *Victory* logbook.

The collector left us alone for several minutes in a cold, dank waiting area before he bustled in with a padded envelope. No small talk. No offer of tea or coffee, despite the collective 15,000 miles travelled by his guests. I thought his movements swift for a man of his age, like a retired dancer. There was something of a side samba in his step.

'That's the Nelson,' he mumbled, sliding the envelope across the table. 'I've had it fifty years. One of a kind. Did you know HMS *Victory*'s the one surviving ship to have par-ticipated in the American War of Independence?'

'I didn't know that,' I said. 'Amazing.'

Razi suddenly took a hand to his face and started rubbing one of his cheeks. 'Shucks. In all honesty, I should keep it. I must be crazy to let it go.'

My heart sank. I thought of the dozens of emails and phone calls over the previous three months trying to convince this guy to sell; the twelve-hour flight.

'Well, from what I hear, it's going to a great home,' I said, carefully eyeing my French colleague, who was the one with the actual client buying this thing. Buying it for half a million pounds.

'Yes. Absolutely,' she said, smiling tightly.

The New Yorker seemed unperturbed by the change in mood.

'It's a great item, Johnny,' he half shouted. 'And you're getting a great price.'

'I know, I know,' said Razi. 'You're right. It's just . . . I never expected to sell it – that's all. I'm not fickle like some collectors. But I guess at my age you do have to think about selling a few things.' He looked mighty worried for all of two seconds, then his expression cleared up. 'I also have Nelson's last letter to Emma Hamilton if you're interested?'

The logbook was authentic, alright – we leafed through. It was written in Nelson's crooked hand, no question, the admiral's daily autograph annotations about weather, wind speed, location. We signed the paperwork, none that mentioned the final selling price nor any aspect of the three dealers' varying commission rates. Meanwhile, the Iranian owner stood fidgeting, apparently wrestling with himself to change his mind, or perhaps still worrying about the outcome of the Battle of Trafalgar.

I returned to the resort hotel with the heavy wooden interior suggestive of a hunting lodge. Really, it catered to golf fanatics – ancient ones – who rode up and down in carts out back. I caught some sun by the pool. One more day here before returning to London. The cheery waiter from breakfast, the one with the overdeveloped smile muscles, brought me an Old Fashioned. Now, who did he remind me of? The one from *Chips* with all the teeth. Erik something. Estrada – that was it.

'Here's to the first of the day!' the waiter laughed, entering into an odd bow.

He needn't have bothered. I'd already tipped him.

The Americans unfurled themselves around me on sunbeds and talked golf scores while I stared up at the sky and tried a daydream. I spooled through my autograph victories to date: a Van Gogh letter, a Churchill love note, a Karl Marx, a Rasputin. But something else kept creeping into view, narrowing my focus, something producing a sourness that drained away even this sun-drenched scene. An age-old doubt about this career of mine, a hard-to-shake disapproval of the mechanics of collecting, my facilitation of it; a feeling that I must be crazy myself to be professionally surrounded by this many lunatics. Thirty-eight years old, and still in my father's orbit.

§

2012 had been the year of Adrian's cancer. At the age of sixty-eight, the exact same age his father had died, he developed throat cancer. Adrian, who had never smoked and was teetotal. He and I were side by side in the consultant's office on Harley Street when the word "malignant" was uttered. The prognosis was good – he was on the lucky side of things – but the treatment would be aggressive: two rounds of radiotherapy, plus chemo.

We went for sandwiches at the Langham Hotel in Regent Street straight afterwards, and were joined by my father's now wife, Giorgia. She and I were possessed by nervous energy; after sandwiches, we made inroads into a pile of scones. Adrian didn't eat a morsel. He sat quietly surveying the scene from the corner of an enormous armchair, as if viewing everything from the wrong end of a telescope.

'I can't believe it,' he said, eventually. 'Cancer.'

*

The radiotherapy took its toll, wore my father down, transformed him into a sick old man, mostly through weight loss; he had so little fat to spare at the start. My mother asked after him, sent her best wishes. She said she was very sad to hear about it but didn't feel comfortable getting in touch. My sister and I visited him at his flat, played the devoted son and daughter. Ruth had two children now, a twelve-year-old and a ten-year-old, Rachel and I had a three-year-old, while Adrian and Giorgia had a five-year-old son of their own. That final grenade flung by Adrian at the old life; at my sister and me; at my mother.

The radiotherapy was worse than advertised. Adrian ended up hospitalized. He lay in bed at the Royal Marsden, a wreck of a man. I sat watching him as he got quieter and quieter. Then there was the day he could only nod.

'Remember our trip to California in 1981?' I asked.

My father nodded his head.

'How we saw those autographs in cement? At Grauman's Chinese Theatre? I wonder if that's what gave me the idea. It's thirty years ago, but for some reason I keep remembering how you drove us around California, the four of us. I suppose it was a happy time.'

Another nod.

'Are you feeling sick?'

My father pulled himself up out of bed. It looked like it took a huge effort. I helped him to his feet, then supported him to the sink, where he began to retch horribly. I rubbed his back as he spat out the vomit, felt the painful struggle of it vibrating against my palms. I could feel his ribs. Then I helped him back into bed. He was even more tired now, and shut his eyes, but I sensed his wish to remain awake.

'It's strange that I ended up in autographs, don't you think?' I said. 'Feels like a weird accident. I understand the entrepreneur bit – I was being like Grandpa. But the rest is mysterious. It wasn't a career I expected.'

I thought of Jožka now, dead for all of four years. He made it to ninety-four in the end, with all his marbles, plus the girlfriend. As gracious an exit as anyone could hope for.

Now I'd brought up my career, I thought cursorily about the other parts of my life my father knew nothing about, those bits that didn't feature in our relationship, didn't fit: the club nights in Ibiza, books, ideas, a thousand nights of laughter and conversation with friends. In that other version of my life, the version I'd actually lived, the celebrity names and ink on paper were just details – a means to an end, a living. Yet, in this father–son world of ours, collecting took centre stage; it was most of what we talked about. A complicated piece of legislation that could never be fully passed.

My father didn't move his head this time. Perhaps he was thinking of Jožka, whom he loved – he always said so. Or maybe he didn't have the energy to nod. There was very little trace of Adrian left, actually. His hair was thinning – just a few wisps of white. His trademark energy had faded. If I were to put a pen in his hand, could he still do his ridiculous squiggle, I wondered? The self-important flourish at the end of business letters, while Trisha typed in the background. 'Why can't you write your name so people can read it?' my mother used to ask him. I thought of my own splat on the page that refused to be Adam Andrusier. My autograph spoke of refusal, avoidance, aspiration – just like Adrian's.

'If you're tired,' I said, 'I can just sit here with you.'

Again, no response. I took out my newspaper and sat reading. Every now and then I took a peek at my father. He wasn't asleep. His eyes were open. He was having thoughts. Then I put down the newspaper and joined him in his silence. I concentrated on imbibing the physical sensation of being in a room with Adrian, the organic matter of him. I might need this memory, I thought; I might really need it. Then I wondered if there was anything special to say, any unfinished business that needed covering. In fact, it was enough just being here, facing this nebulous thing together in the Royal Marsden, facing the strange possibility of an ending. And with no interruption. Not a single one of my father's jokes, or 'now, that reminds me' or 'I must just tell you' or getting everything wrong. Just the two of us in a room. If only I could bottle this silence, I thought.

Adrian was with his father when he died. He described it to me a couple of times. 'At the end, he took in a deep breath then let it out slowly,' he said, 'and that was it. It was awful.' Adrian was nineteen when that happened. He was also the one with Grandma Lotka when she died. My mother and grandfather couldn't face it, so Adrian offered. He could face it. He sat with Lotka during her last breath. He said the same thing happened: a big inhalation of breath that was let out slowly.

'I should probably get back home now,' I said.

My father's eyes described an arc up to the ceiling and across to his son. His eldest son. The one from earlier. It's good night from me, and it's good night from him. The hospital door clicked shut behind me.

§

I decided, before dinner, to take a drive up into the dusty mountains near San Diego, the Palomar loop route. It looked like a beautiful evening up ahead. I wound my way along the tree-rimmed highway, up into the mountain-tops, finally through to a clearing where Lake Henshaw reflected the pink of the sky. The scene was stunning, but I couldn't concentrate. Famous names and faces kept going through my head, like the conveyor belt on the *Generation Game*. The people I'd met – the Yeltsins, the Ray Charleses, the Liz Taylors – and the people I'd sold. And I kept being pulled back to that trip to California in 1981; something nudging me there.

Perhaps my father had driven us down this very road, I speculated, my sister and I in the back, my mother in the front beside him, a sweet-sour sixties number streaming through on the hi-fi. My father was probably giving his talk about America being the land of opportunity where all the best entertainment was made. We had those cardboard cut-outs of Charles and Diana in the back windows, the happy royal couple with moving hands that waved; bought in Hamleys, installed by Adrian. The Americans stopped in the streets and stared and pointed. Some waved obediently. 'My God, is that Prince Edward?' a man shouted, clamping his mouth in shock. Dad wound down his window and slowed the car to offer a correction. Or maybe he was making the other speech, the one about the members of his family that travelled to America from Russia a hundred years earlier. He had literally no idea where they might be now – for all he knew, they'd ended up as top executives at the studios.

'There's no reason to think that,' said my mother.

*

The sun was starting to set, so I stopped to get an obligatory picture of the lake. I rarely took photos. One shot for every ten thousand taken by my father in the eighties. I had to remember to take pictures the way some people had to remember to take their medication. Rachel mostly reminded me, when our son's face was covered in bolognese, or he was dancing in his nappy and wellington boots. 'Take a picture. Quick.' My iPhone made the photograph sound now, and I tried texting it to Rachel, then to my father. No reception.

§

Two months after the Royal Marsden and the birds were tweeting again in Hampstead Village. I was walking through on the way to my dad's place when I noticed some flash photography outside the Flask pub. I recognized the face. A handsome young Hollywood star. But, wait. No one was asking for an autograph! That seemed odd. The group of swooning young girls around him had no interest in the way the actor might write his name – no one searching for pen and paper. They were handing him their phones instead, one by one, and placing their faces next to his for selfies. Uploaded within the hour, I presumed. What was it: Instagram?

I descended the stairs to my father's flat and paused to watch through the window above the door as my father's regrown brush of white curls darted between kitchen and living area. Then I knocked twice and waited.

'Come in, my son,' Adrian said, scampering away from the doorway, a magnifying glass in his hand.

His white hair disappeared into the next room, and I followed him down into his rabbit hole.

Sixties music blaring, and the sofa covered with wide-open collectors' albums and a book entitled *The Synagogues of Ukraine*. Adrian was home alone. His Facebook page was open on the computer screen in the corner. The mantelpiece was now deluged with photographs. The ones of me and Ruth were relegated towards the back. My father's new son took pride of place now: a sweet, skinny, brown-haired child. The various scenarios of this little boy's childhood looked remarkably similar to mine: eating ice cream on a beach, perched on Adrian's shoulders with a Venice backdrop, in a pushchair outside Kenwood House. Same situations; some differences in personnel. It made me think again of the photographic composites my father created in the study in Pinner. His new son's head on his first son's body, his new wife mapped onto Anna.

'I've found an amazing card,' said Adrian, looking straight through me, eyes like pins, and with that special urgent vibrato of his, reserved for Holocaust-themed discussion. 'I must just show you.'

'Sure. What is it, Dad?'

'Something unbelievable. A picture of the Jewish ghetto police in Lvov. I think it must be unique. Never seen anything like it. I'm going to put it up on Facebook later.'

A row of uniformed men stared uncertainly at the camera.

'Amazing,' I said.

Adrian tapped the photo and smiled at his good fortune.

'You seem so much better, Dad.'

'I feel fine,' he said. 'I even went Israeli dancing last night. I'm getting my energy back. But the whole thing has been awful.'

'Yes. You were in a terrible state.'

My father flicked a smile, and I detected a defensiveness. He didn't want to think about illness any more, could no longer contemplate that kind of defeat.

'You remember that time you came to visit me in hospital?' he asked. 'When I was so weak? Well, that was the very worst day of all. I didn't even have the energy to talk. I wanted so much to speak, but I couldn't.'

'Oh,' I said. 'I didn't realize that.'

My father turned his attention back to the card, held up his magnifying glass and squinted. Finally, he put it down in his lap, blinked his eyes, and said, 'How's Mummy?'

§

After my stop at Lake Henshaw, I turned the car around and drifted back into 1981.

'Charles and Diana have been a hit!' my father from that time shouted, above the drone of the music. 'Really *successful*. Are you having a wonderful time, childries?' He eyed us in the rear-view mirror.

'Yeeeeeees!' my sister and I shouted.

'People react to these cut-outs as if they're real,' mused Mum. 'It's bizarre.'

'See if you like this,' said Dad. 'The Mamas and the Papas.'

'California Dreamin'' drifted through the speakers. I'd never heard it before, but it sounded urgent – neither happy nor sad. Dad explained, again, that one of the singers was Mama Cass, who had been enormously overweight and Jewish.

'We know,' my sister shouted.

'Died at the age of thirty-two,' said Dad, turning down the volume. 'Choked on a sandwich.'

We drove to Los Angeles from San Francisco, which had the crookedest street in the world and a view of Alcatraz from our hotel window. My father pointed towards it every day.

'Alcatraz housed some of the most notorious criminals in US history,' he read to us from the guidebook, 'the most famous of which was Al Capone.' Then he closed the book and said, 'You should see the Clint Eastwood film. It's fantastic.'

Now, cruising through Beverly Hills, my father twisting the star map in his lap – each famous person's house marked with a gold star. We drove past Mel Brooks's place, and Clint Eastwood's and Sinatra's. I'd never heard that word before. Sinatra. He slowed the car and we passed by a pair of ornate golden gates, trees and greenery obscuring the view beyond.

'This one,' he shouted. 'This is it!' as if he'd discovered the place where his long-lost relatives lived – the ones who'd moved to America from Russia a hundred years earlier and disappeared without a trace.

'Elvis lived here!'

Spindly gates this time, and a tradesman's lorry parked up on the drive. Clanging jewellery and pointy hairdos drifted into my thoughts, and my mother saying, 'Elvis was very handsome.'

We stopped the car at Grauman's Chinese Theatre next, and my father showed us all the signatures in the concrete.

'Wow, Marilyn Monroe,' he said.

I stared at the writing, encrusted in rock – like the tablets of stone given by God to Moses. It gave me a strange feeling in my stomach.

'You know her real name was Norma Jeane.'

'Was it?'

'And Garbo's real name was Greta Gustafsson, I think.'

I imagined Marilyn pausing for thought when she signed her name, having to pretend to be Marilyn when she was really Norma Jeane.

'And look! Liz Taylor,' said Adrian.

I looked at the big elaborate 'T' in the famous name, and the date above: 1956.

'Ruth's tired,' said my mother. 'I think it's probably enough now.'

'Wait a minute. Wait a minute. We need to find Danny Kaye. His real name was Daniel Kaminski, you know.'

We visited Universal Studios and went on a special open-top bus, which took you on a tour of the best special effects. We drove alongside a lake and a huge plastic shark came out of the water, right up to our bus – the model they'd used in *Jaws*, which I was too young to see. Everyone screamed and laughed. My father cheerfully stroked my mother's cheek. Then there was a bit where I got to fly like Superman. I lay down on a bed on a raised platform with a huge cinema screen behind me that showed sky and clouds, and they projected an image of me up onto the screen, somehow making the bed invisible, and making me look as if I was flying.

'My boy is Superman,' he said, after I'd had my turn. And I felt like I really was. My father stroked my cheeks, and it was as if the moment would last forever.

§

I made it back to the hotel at around 8 p.m., dizzied by the drive and the memories of 1981. I wondered if I'd spent a lifetime trying to get there – to the back of that hire car, beside my sister and behind my parents. What an elaborate thing to do. And for what purpose? Or maybe we all did something like that: built versions of ourselves to obfuscate the losses.

The moon was bright and the sea purred. I got out of my car and walked along the path opposite my hotel, which looked down onto a palm-fringed bay. And who should be walking towards me? A man of about my father's age, with a deep receding hairline and pink-lensed Ray-Bans sitting up on his forehead. Only Jack Nicholson. But was it, though? It seemed far-fetched. I couldn't be sure. He was all alone, walking with his hands held behind his back. And, wait, he caught my eye. We were looking right at each other, so I stopped still.

'Nice night for it,' he said.

'It is. Yes.'

He sniffed in a deep lungful of evening sea air and stood right next to me, looking out at the horizon. Was it really him? I could ask for an autograph and find out. But it was too perfect a situation for a thing like that; us standing there, side by side, staring into the night.

'Now, are you who I think you are?' I asked eventually. I smiled and half winked.

The man turned and smiled back, more to himself than at me. So Nicholson.

'I'm his brother,' he said.

Did Nicholson even have a brother? I didn't think so. I remembered that line, suddenly, from *Chinatown*. 'To tell you the truth, I lied a little.'

We both laughed, the sea swooshed and the waves crashed. The moonlight picked out the crests of the waves below in a bluish tinge. With this guy by my side, the sounds of the sea swelled louder and louder, growing steadily into a round of rapturous applause.

Acknowledgements

An enormous thank you and body-slam of a hug to Josh Appignanesi for his loving input, incisive brain and generous encouragement throughout the writing of this book, including that time I first mentioned the idea during drinks in the old life, in the bowels of Camden.

A huge thank you to Stephen Howard for insisting this was a good idea right from the start. Thank you to Taymour Soomro for his relentless encouragement and honesty. Thank you to Michael Worrell for really listening and letting me repeat myself so many times. Thank you to Vaughan Pilikian for helping me assert my identity as a writer. Thank you to Nick Laird for saying, 'Make it about you. Set it in Pinner.' Thank you, Zadie Smith, for telling me to keep writing all those years ago, and for supporting this book so wholeheartedly.

I also need to thank Devorah Baum for her tireless support, and for always knowing what I mean about everything (even when I don't); Judith Clark, for her careful reading and friendship; Adam Rosenthal, for so many positive noises over the years; Caroline Howard, for the discussions over coffee, all her reading, and for her continuously insightful feedback; and Adam Phillips, for drawing my attention to the intense pleasure of writing.

Gratitude to my agent, Jonny Geller, for believing in this book, and being so nice. Also, to Viola Hayden, for feedback and belief. And to my editor, Fiona Crosby, who seems to love this book in the exact way I could ever have hoped and dreamed.

Thank you to my mother – for her fierce intellect, for her unswerving attention when I was young, for her infinite interest in what lies beneath surfaces.

Thank you to my father for his generosity – including his big-hearted reaction to this book – and his indefatigable enthusiasm for life.

Thank you to my sister for being the truest possible companion throughout childhood. I could write an entire other book about the fun we had, the worlds we created, the experiences we shared.

Thank you to Rachel, who is the best friend anyone could ever hope for, who has weathered too many storms with me, who only ever wants the best for me, who can hear anything and see through everything.

And thank you, Jacob, for filling my life with joy.

Epigraph Sources

RONNIE BARKER: *Sauce*, 1977.

BIG DADDY: Quoted in Ryan Danes, *Who's the Daddy: The Life and Times of Shirley Crabtree*, 2013.

SINATRA: Letter to Nancy Sinatra, 1969, quoted in Nancy Sinatra, *Frank Sinatra: An American Legend*, 1995.

RAY CHARLES: *Brother Ray: Ray Charles' Own Story*, with David Ritz, 2003, p.174.

MILES DAVIS: Interview with Hollie West in the *Washington Post*, March 1969.

NELSON MANDELA: From his 'Address in Capetown', the first speech he made upon being released from prison at the Parade Cape Town, 9 February 1990.

RICHARD GERE: Documentary interview with *Project Happiness*, 2012.

BORIS YELTSIN: Televised speech, 4 October 1993.

STEVE REICH: *Writings on Music 1965–2000*, with Paul Hillier, 2002, p.20.

SALMAN RUSHDIE: *Imaginary Homelands: Essays and Criticism 1981–1991*, 1992, p.12.

HARRY SECOMBE: *The Goon Show*, 17 January 1956.

JAWS: Interview with Universal Exports, 2002.

MARILYN: Interview in *Time* magazine, 17 August 1962.

ELVIS: Interview in Los Angeles, 28 October 1957.

HITLER: From *The Producers*, Mel Brooks, 1967.

MONICA LEWINSKY: Encounter at LAX Airport, 1999.

Synagoge Prinzregentenstra

jüdische Synagoge
Lublinitz O/S.